THE GREAT BOOK OF FLORIDA

The Crazy History of Florida with
Amazing Random Facts & Trivia

**A Trivia Nerds Guide
to the History of the
United States Vol.4**

BILL O'NEILL

DON'T FORGET YOUR FREE BOOKS

CONTENTS

CHAPTER TWO
FLORIDA'S POP CULTURE 27

CHAPTER THREE
FACTS ABOUT FLORIDA'S ATTRACTIONS 53

CHAPTER FOUR
FLORIDA'S INVENTIONS, IDEAS, AND MORE! ...74

CHAPTER FIVE
FLORIDA'S BIGGEST HAUNTS, SUPERNATURAL,
AND OTHER WEIRD FACTS...................................... 97

INTRODUCTION

What do you really know about the state of Florida?

Sure, just about everyone knows that Florida is home to Walt Disney World and Universal Studios. You probably know that it's one of the most popular tourist states in America. But what else do you *really* know about the Sunshine State?

Have you ever wondered how Florida got its name or what it means?

Do you know which nicknames are commonly used to describe Floridians?

You know by now that Florida experiences a lot of hurricanes, but do you know how many the state has been affected by?

Do you know which legendary singer had his first indoor concert *ever* in Florida and why it was a controversial event at the time?

Do you know what unsolved mysteries have taken place in the state? Have you heard about any of the state's most haunted spots?

Today, it's home to a number of theme parks. Do you know what the very first theme park is? Do you know what attraction is considered to be the oldest in Florida?

Do you know which famous sports drink was invented in Florida and why? Do you know which protective skin care product came from the state?

If you have ever wondered about the answers to these or other questions, then you've come to the right place. This book is packed with stories and facts about the state of Florida.

This isn't just any book about the Sunshine State. We'll take a closer look at some of the facts that have helped shape Florida into the state it is today. You'll learn more than you ever could have wondered. Once you're done reading, you'll feel like a Florida expert! You'll be sure to impress your history teacher.

This book is broken up into easy to follow chapters that will help you learn more about the Sunshine State. After you have finished reading each chapter, you can test your knowledge with trivia questions!

Some of the facts you'll read in this book are bound to surprise you. Others are sad, some are strange, and some might creep you out a little. But the one thing that each of the facts in this book have in common is that they're *all* interesting!

The book will answer the following questions:

How did Florida get its name?

Which former U.S. president helped the country gain control of Florida?

Which city in Florida was the only city in America to be founded by a woman?

How did spring break get started?

What famous pirates buried treasure on and off the coast of Florida?

How did Walt Disney keep his plans to build Disney World a secret?

Which of the Disney World attractions is said to be haunted?

What lighthouse is thought to be one of America's most haunted?

And so much more!

CHAPTER ONE

FLORIDA'S HISTORY'S HISTORY AND RANDOM FACTS

Florida was the 27th state to join the United States. Do you know how it got its name or which country once had control over the territory before it became part of the U.S.? Do you know why its state nickname is misleading? Do you know which American president helped shape Florida history? One hint: a city in the state is named after him. Do you know what shocking treasure may be found in the state? Read on to find out some of these and other facts!

Florida Was Named After a Holiday

Did you know that Florida is named after a Christian holiday? One hint: it's *not* Christmas—even though there is a Christmas Tree Island in the Florida Keys.

Florida was named after Easter!

In 1513, Spanish explorer Juan Ponce de León arrived

in the area that would become Saint Augustine. He made it to the area shortly after the Easter holiday. When Ponce de León named the area, he chose to honor both the holiday and the colorful plant life he found in the region. Ponce de León chose to name the land "Pascua Florida," a Spanish phrase for the Easter season. This translates to "feast of flowers."

The state's name is the oldest place-name with European origins in the United States. Florida was also the first region in the continental United States to have ever been visited by Europeans.

St. Augustine is the Oldest European-Established Settlement in the USA

St. Augustine was founded in 1565 by Spanish explorers. It's the oldest city in Florida that has been continuously occupied by Europeans. There are a number of well-preserved historical sites in the city, such as Flagler College and a few forts.

St. Augustine also has a history as capital in the state. When the region was under Spanish control, St. Augustine was its capital for more than 200 years. When the Territory of Florida was established, St. Augustine remained its capital. In 1824, however, the capital was moved to Tallahassee—where it has remained ever since!

Today, St. Augustine is a major tourist attraction. This

is largely thanks to the city's rich history, but it also plenty of things to see and do. From its lighthouse and beaches to its ghost tours and the St. Augustine Pirate and Treasure Museum, you won't get bored!

A Former President Helped the United States Gain Control of Florida

Did you know that before he became president of the United States, Andrew Jackson was busy shaping Florida's history?

Andrew Jackson led the First Seminole War. His excursions took place in West Florida and Spanish Florida against the Seminole Indians. While Great Britain and Spain were both outraged by the attacks, Spain was unable to defend its territory. Spain ended up ceding Florida to the United States through the Adams-Onis Treaty, otherwise known as the Transcontinental Treaty or the Florida Purchase Treaty, in 1819.

The United States named the region the Territory of Florida. When it was established in 1821, General Andrew Jackson was appointed the territory's first military governor (not to be confused with Florida state governor). The city of Jacksonville was also named after Andrew Jackson.

But Slavery Almost Prevented Florida From Becoming a State

After the Territory of Florida was established, the state's population increased during that time to the point where it was large enough to become a state. The only problem? Slavery was allowed in Florida. Most of the northern states didn't want another pro-slave state to become a part of the Union.

So, how *did* Florida end up becoming a state, even though it remained a pro-slavery state? Well, you can thank it all on Iowa. It was decided that Iowa, which was a non-slavery state at the time, would help balance out the difference. Both Florida and Iowa became a part of the United States on March 3, 1845.

Of course, Florida's status as a pro-slavery state did cause problems later down the road. The state seceded from the Union and join the Confederacy. Florida also played a key role in the Civil War. It acted as a supply route for the Confederate Army during the Civil War. There were a lot of smaller battles fought when the Union tried to blockade the state in order to prevent supplies from reaching the Confederates.

Florida rejoined the Union in 1868 after the Civil War ended.

Florida's State Nickname Just Might Fool You

Thanks to most of the state's humid subtropical

climate, which has attracted vacationers for decades, Florida was nicknamed the "Sunshine State." But did you know the state's nickname is actually sort of misleading?

When you hear the "Sunshine State," you might assume that it's the sunniest state in the country. While Florida might have ideal weather, you might be surprised to learn that it's actually *not* the sunniest state in the country. That title would go to Arizona and then to Nevada, which means that Florida is only the third sunniest state in the U.S.A.

Florida has a number of unofficial state nicknames, some of which may be more fitting than its actual nickname. These include:

- The Alligator State
- The Everglade State
- The Orange State
- The Flower State
- The Peninsula State
- The Gulf State

Florida is a Space Capital of the United States

NASA's John F. Kennedy Space Center and the Cape Canaveral Air Force Station are both located in Florida. In fact, Florida is considered the United States' primary launch pad for both aeronautic testing and space flights.

Unsurprisingly, Florida is also rich in space history. Since 1968, more than 100 space shuttle missions have been launched out of NASA's Kennedy Space Center. The Apollo and Skylab operations are the most well-known.

Some of the biggest space events of all time also started out in the state. In 1962, John Glenn became the first American to orbit the Earth when he launched from Cape Canaveral. In 1969, Neil Armstrong became the first man to walk on the moon after Apollo 11 was launched from the Kennedy Space Center.

In the 1960s, NASA also built a rocket testing facility in Homestead, Florida. While the project was discontinued, the government chose to leave the site. A rocket can still be found there today!

The Florida Keys Once Declared War on the Rest of the United States

Did you know that the Florida Keys seceded from the United States back in 1982 for all of two minutes? It also declared war on the rest of the country.

Declaring their independence, they named themselves the Conch Republic. They did this as part of an effort to protest a roadblock in Florida City that had been established by the Border Patrol. Mayor Dennis Wardlow, who gave himself the name of Prime Minister of the Conch Republic, declared war against the United States. Wardlow surrendered two minutes later and requested $1 million in foreign aid.

While the secession was unsuccessful, Key West is still commonly referred to as the Conch Republic today!

The First American Christmas Took Place in Florida

With its palm trees, sandy beaches, and unlikely chance of snow, Florida might seem like the least likely locale for America's first Christmas to be held. And yet, the first American Christmas on record took place in the Sunshine State!

According to historians, the first American Christmas took place in Tallahassee in 1539. It was celebrated by Spanish explorer and conquistador Hernando de Soto and other members of his expedition, who were staying near the Historic Capitol of downtown Tallahassee.

Ancient artifacts were discovered during a church excavation, which helped historians understand how, exactly, the first Christmas was celebrated. It was quite different from the Christmas most Americans think of today. There were no presents or Christmas trees or lights. There were no stockings, candy canes or snowmen. The holiday involved a religious observance with a Christmas mass. Women cooked for the holiday. Pig bones were discovered, which led historians to believe the Spanish were the first to bring pigs to Florida. Historians also believe local fruits, vegetables, and seafood were incorporated in the Christmas meal.

Tourism in Florida Began *Before* Disney World Opened

You might think Walt Disney World is what originally began to draw tourists to Florida and for good reason. Today, Disney World is the most visited amusement park in the world. It draws in more than 16 million tourists each year. However, tourism to Florida was popular even before Disney World opened!

Tourists first began to take interest in Florida in the late 19th century when Henry Flagler built the Florida East Coast Railway, which ran from Jacksonville to Key West. The trip included a number of luxurious hotels throughout the route, such as the Ponce de Leon Hotel in St. Augustine and the Royal Palm Hotel in Miami.

Tourist interest in the state really ignited in 1888 when President Grover Cleveland and the first lady took a trip to the state. He visited Jacksonville, St. Augustine, and Winter Park, to name a few locations. While he was in Jacksonville, Cleveland made a speech in support of tourism to Florida.

In the 1930s, Florida saw its first theme parks. The

very first theme park to open in Florida was Cypress Gardens. Marineland came shortly after.

It wasn't until 1971 that Magic Kingdom, the first Disney theme park in Orlando, opened.

Miami Was the Only City in America to be Founded by a Woman

Did you know that only one city in the entire country was founded by a woman and it just so happens to be in Florida?

Back in 1874, a woman from Cleveland named Julia Tuttle visited her father, who lived in the area. After her father left his land to her when he died, she decided to buy more property. She then talked Henry Flagler into extending his railway to the area.

By the 1920s, Miami had become a bustling metropolitan area—and it was all thanks to Tuttle, who today is known as the "Mother of Miami."

A 10-foot statue of Julia Tuttle was built in Bayfront Park in 2010.

Florida Has More Hurricanes Than Any Other State in the Country

By now, you probably know that Florida is often affected by hurricanes. But did you know that it's had more hurricanes than any other U.S. state?

As of 2017, Florida has been affected by 117 hurricanes.

That's nearly *double* the number of hurricanes as Texas, which has had the second highest number of hurricanes in the country.

Interestingly, Florida hurricanes tend to occur more often during even years—though hurricanes have occurred in odd years as well. Florida has had over 60 hurricanes occur during even years and more than 50 during odd years.

While there have been years in which the state wasn't hit by a hurricane, multiple hurricanes have taken place other years. The highest number of hurricanes in the state occurred during 2005. Fifteen hurricanes took place that year.

Pirates Buried Their Treasure in Florida

If you're hoping to find some buried pirate treasure, you might want to head to the sunshine state. According to researchers and historians, Florida is home to more buried treasure than any other U.S. state. In fact, it's been estimated that $165 million worth of treasure was buried on or off the coasts of Florida.

In 2015, divers found $4.5 million worth of gold coins off the coast of Vero Beach.

Some of the most well-known pirates in history are said to have buried their treasure in Florida. Some of these include Blackbeard, Henri "Black Caesar"

Caesar, Kidd, Bowlegs, Bonnett, Lafitte, and Jose "Gasparilla" Gaspar. These pirates would roam the Caribbean Sea and seize other ships. They would then bury their steals on the shores of Florida. When the pirates died, so did the whereabouts of their buried treasures.

There are a number of popular legends about pirate treasure buried in Florida.

Gasparilla's headquarters were at Boca Grande, which is today called Gasparilla Island. He looted what is estimated to have been worth $30 million. He had hundreds of crew members, who also buried their treasures on the islands.

Blackbeard is said to have buried $2,000 near the Boca Raton inlet. It's also been rumored that the famous pirate buried some of his treasures near Miami, too.

It's also been said that there's treasure that ended up getting lost at sea off the southwest coast of Florida. The legend goes like this: when King Phillip of Spain married Isabella Farnese, the Duchess of Parma, in 1713, she requested unique jewels before consummating their marriage. King Phillip commissioned jewels for her, including a 74-carat emerald ring, more than 40 chests of emeralds, and a jewel-studded carriage. The treasure was lost off the southwest coast of Florida during a storm.

The Tampa Bay area is also rumored to be home to

buried pirate treasure.

Spring Break Started Out Because of a College Professor's Book

Daytona Beach may be the most famous place in Florida for spring breakers, but it might surprise you to learn that it's actually *not* where spring break started out. It actually began in Fort Lauderdale.

It all started out in 1935 when Colgate University's swim team went to practice in Fort Lauderdale over winter break. This led to an annual aquatic conference, which drew in students who were not involved with swimming.

Three years later, a college professor from the university named Glendon Swarthout heard about a trip his students were taking to Fort Lauderdale. He decided to join them on the trip and then published a book titled *Where the Boys Are*. The book was turned into a popular movie and a song. The following year, 50,000 students headed to Fort Lauderdale to take part in spring break.

During the late 1980s, Fort Lauderdale added some restrictions to stop spring break partygoers. They raised the drinking age, open containers became illegal, and a wall was built to separate the beach from the road.

By 1985, students had made their way to Daytona

Beach for spring break. Daytona saw more than 300,000 students during spring break that year. The city was initially resistant to spring break. There was a crackdown on bars and clubs, and hundreds of students were arrested. This drove spring breakers to Panama City Beach. Both Daytona Beach and Panama City Beach remain popular spring break destinations today, however.

There's an Annual Dead Fish Toss in Florida

One of the biggest beach parties in the country is held at the Flora-Bama Beach Bar in Pensacola every April. It's called the Interstate Mullet Toss, and it's pretty... well, *weird*.

Thousands of people stand at the Florida state line with dead mullets (a type of fish that's common in the area), which they toss into Alabama. There's a competition to see whose dead mullet gets tossed the furthest. And it's all for a good cause—approximately $40,000 gets raised for charities in both Florida and Alabama each year!

People come from all around the world to participate in the event!

The Black Lives Matter Movement Started Out Due to a Florida Murder Case

By now, you've probably heard of the Black Lives Matter movement, which started out back in 2013. But did you know that it all started out because of a murder that took place in Florida?

In 2012, George Zimmerman shot and killed a 17-year-old African-American Trayvon Martin. The shooting occurred in the Retreat at Twin Lakes community in Sanford, Florida, of which Zimmerman was a neighborhood watch coordinator.

Zimmerman made a phone call to the police, who arrived shortly after he fatally shot Martin.

Zimmerman claimed that he shot Martin in self-defense. He was released from police custody just five hours after the shooting because there was no evidence to suggest he was lying. Under Florida Statute, it was illegal for police to make an arrest. They also said it was within Zimmerman's rights to defend himself with lethal force.

However, George Zimmerman was still charged with murder.

The trial took place in 2013, during which the jury acquitted George Zimmerman of second-degree murder and manslaughter. The Department of Justice also determined that there was no evidence of a hate crime.

People throughout America were outraged by this decision, leading them to use the hashtag #BlackLivesMatter on social media networks.

This is what jumpstarted the movement, which has been one of the most controversial movements throughout the United States.

RANDOM FACTS

1. A lot of people live in Florida. As of 2014, Florida is the state with the 3rd largest population in America. The Sunshine State is home to nearly 20 million residents! Less than 200,000 of those residents live in the state's capital, Tallahassee. People are also constantly migrating to the state. In fact, it's been estimated that approximately 1,000 people move to Florida on a daily basis. According to moving.com, Jacksonville ranked at No. 12 and Miami ranks at No. 44 on the largest cities by U.S. population list. Surprisingly, no Florida cities fall into the top 10!

2. Miami got its name from the Mayaimi Indians, who built villages near Lake Okeechobee and lived in the area until the late 17th century. The tribe named themselves after the word they used for Lake Okeechobee. The word "Mayaimi" translates to "big water." With Miami Beach and Biscayne Bay, this seems like a fitting name for the city. And Miami's not the only city that got its name from the Native Americans. The name "Tampa" is believed to have meant "sticks of fire" in the Calusa Indian language. It was likely given to the city due to its frequent lightning. Florida's

state capital, Tallahassee, originated from the Muskogean Indian language. It translates to "old fields."

3. Key West has the highest average temperatures in the United States. The coolest month is January, which averages highs of 75° Fahrenheit, while August sees the hottest average temps: highs of 91° Fahrenheit.

4. Florida is a really flat state. In fact, it's the flattest state in the entire country. While people often assume that Kansas is the flattest state, Florida actually has the smallest difference between its high and low points, making it even flatter. There's only a 345-foot difference in elevation across the state. The state's mean elevation is only 100 feet.

5. There are a number of different nicknames for Floridians. Thanks to the state's alligator population, Floridians are sometimes referred to as "Alligators." They've also been called "Crackers," a nickname that stemmed from the mule-drivers cracking whips in the 1800s. Floridians have also been known as "Fly-Up-The-Creeks" because of a type of Green Heron that was common in the marshy shorelines of the Sunshine State.

6. Florida is the leading state in citrus fruit production. In fact, it's been estimated that 70% of America's oranges come from the Sunshine State.

Worldwide, Brazil and China are the only places that produce more citrus fruits than Florida.

7. Florida was once known as the "Lightning Capital of the World," but NASA later discovered that the country of Rwanda was more prone to lightning strikes. However, Florida is home to the most lightning strikes in the United States. While Tampa is known as the "Lightning Capital of the World" (or, more accurately, in the United States), Daytona Beach, Fort Myers, Key West, Miami, Orlando, and Tallahassee are almost some of the most lightning-strike prone cities in the U.S. It's been estimated that approximately 10 people are killed and 30 people are injured by lightning in Florida every year.

8. You might think that the nickname "Venice of America" goes to Venice, Florida, but you couldn't be more wrong. Fort Lauderdale, Florida has been nicknamed the "Venice of America." The city has more than 300 miles of inland waterways that can be navigated by boat.

9. Florida is the only state in all of the U.S. that has two rivers that share the same name. There's a Withlacoochee River in north central Florida, as well as one in Central Florida. The two rivers are not connected through waterways, nor do they share anything else that would connect them. They just happen to share the same name.

10. More toll roads and bridges can be found in Florida than any other state in the country. According to the *Orlando Sentinel,* there are 719 miles of toll roads in the Sunshine State.

11. There are more varieties of seashells on the beaches of Fort Meyers, Captiva Island, and Sanibel Island, Florida than anywhere else in all of North America. This is due to the curvaceous geography of the area, strong current from the Gulf of Mexico, and the broad undershelf that cause the region to have an overabundance of shells.

12. Like other states, Florida has a number of strange laws. It's illegal to have sex with a porcupine, sell your kids, skateboard without a license or wear a strapless dress if you're a man. If you happen to tie your elephant to a parking meter, it's illegal not to pay for it. It's also apparently illegal to shower naked, which makes you wonder how many Floridians are showering in their bathing suits. Speaking of bathing suits, it's a crime to sing in public while wearing one.

13. Florida shares its state motto with the United States, which has the same motto. It's "In God We Trust."

14. It might surprise you to learn that Florida is *not* the southernmost U.S. state. While it might appear that way on a map, Hawaii is actually the furthest

south. Florida *is* the most southern state in the continental United States, however. Miami is the southernmost major city in the continental United States, while Key West is the southernmost point in the continental U.S.

15. In 1998, a law took effect which requires all of Florida state-funded daycare centers and preschools to play classical music for the kids. When the law was enacted, it was believed the "Mozart effect" would help produce smarter children. Although this theory has since been disproven, the law has yet to change.

16. Florida tested out the first—and *only*— "missile mail" in history. In 1959, 3,000 pieces of mail were delivered by a cruise missile that was fired from an American Navy Submarine. The mail was addressed to President Dwight D. Eisenhower, along with other government officials. The missile was launched from the USS Barbero from its location off the coast of Virginia. Less than half an hour later, it arrived at the Naval Auxiliary Air Station in Mayport, Florida. The mail was sorted through the same way it normally would from a post office in Jacksonville. Even though the operation was considered successful, it was considered too expensive and dangerous.

17. Dinosaur fossils haven't been uncovered in Florida. During the dinosaur age, the entire

peninsula of Florida didn't even exist. It was entirely underwater at the time.

18. Miami has the largest cruise ship port in the entire world! As a result, the city offers the largest number of cruises and is recognized as the "Cruise Capital of the World."

19. Sarasota is known as "Circus City" because it was once used as winter headquarters by the Ringling Brothers and Barnum and Bailey.

20. Siesta Key Beach once won an award for having the whitest sand in the world. The beach has large quantities of pure quartz crystals on its shorelines. This means the sand always stays cool. It's a great beach to visit if you don't want to burn your feet.

Test Yourself – Questions and Answers

1. Florida's name stemmed from which of the following meanings?

   a. Wreaths of flowers
   b. Feast of fish
   c. Feast of flowers

2. Which former American President helped the United States gain control of Florida?

   a. George Washington
   b. Andrew Jackson
   c. Abraham Lincoln

3. Neil Armstrong rode aboard the Apollo 11, which launched from:

   a. Kennedy Space Center
   b. Cape Canaveral Air Force Station

4. The name "Tallahassee" originates from which Native American language?

   a. Cherokee Indian
   b. Muskogean Indian
   c. Lenape Indian

5. Which city is considered the "Venice of Florida"?

   a. Fort Lauderdale
   b. Miami
   c. Tampa

Answers

1. c.
2. b.
3. a.
4. b.
5. a.

CHAPTER TWO

FLORIDA'S POP CULTURE

Florida is a state that's rich in pop culture. Do you know which famous musician held his first indoor concert in Florida? Do you know about the subgenre of music that comes out of Florida or which '90s boyband was formed in the state? Do you know which country duo is named after the state? To find out the answers to these and other random facts, read on!

Elvis Performed His First Indoor Concert in Florida

If you're an Elvis Presley fan, you might be surprised to learn that his first indoor concert was held in Florida. It took place at the Florida Theater in Jacksonville in 1956. Not only is it still one of the most memorable concerts that ever took place in the history of the theater, but it was also somewhat controversial at the time.

In fact, the concert was even featured in *Life* magazine due to the controversy surrounding it. The concert was attended by Juvenile Court Judge Marion Gooding. Gooding monitored the performance to ensure that Elvis's movements remained appropriate. Elvis was warned ahead of time to keep the concert appropriate, so he used his finger in place some of his more sexually suggestive movements during the show—which was considered a success.

A Popular TV Show Focused on Retirees in Florida

There's no doubt that you know by now that Florida is a popular place for retirees, due to the warm weather and lack of state taxes. *The Golden Girls*, which made its debut in 1985, focused on this issue.

The series focused on three women in their golden years: Dorothy (Bea Arthur), Rose (Betty White), and Blanche (Rue McClanahan) and Dorothy's mother, Sophia (Estelle Getty). Thanks to being widowed or divorced, the girls find themselves as roommates due to the high cost of living as a single retired woman.

The show introduced Florida culture to the rest of the world. One such example is the word "lanai." A lanai is a porch or veranda, which may or may not be screened in, with cement floors and an awning.

If you're a fan of the show, one thing that may

surprise you is the house's actual geographical location. Although the address in *The Golden Girls* was 6151 Richmond Street in Miami, the house that's used for exterior shots in the show is actually located at 245 North Saltair Avenue in Los Angeles, California. There are high walls and foliage there to prevent fans from trying to catch a glimpse.

Lots of Celebrities Own Restaurants in Florida

Have you ever wondered what celebrities and celebrity chefs own restaurants in Florida? Well, there are quite a few! Some of the most popular celeb-owned restaurants in the Sunshine State include:

- **Bobby's Burger Palace** – Located at the Dadeland Mall near Miami, Bobby Flay's restaurant offers gourmet burgers and milkshakes and malts (including some with alcohol). The restaurant also offers a frozen cactus margarita bar.
- **Bongos Cuban Café** – This Cuban-themed restaurant is owned by Gloria Estefan and her husband, Emilio. Located in Lake Buena Vista, you'll find everything from Cuban Style French Toast and Cuban Sandwiches on the brunch menu to Cuban Style steaks and Shrimp Criollo on the dinner menu.
- **Emeril's Tchoup Chop**– Celebrity chef Emeril Lagasse's restaurant is located inside the Loews Hotel on South Beach in Miami. The New

Orleans-inspired cuisine is quite popular, so be sure to make reservations ahead of time if you plan to visit.

- **Emeril's Orlando** – The celeb chef's other restaurant can be found in the dining complex that connects Universal Studios Orlando to Universal's Islands of Adventure. You'll find classic Emeril Lagasse dishes, such as roast prime rib po'boy and andouille gumbo, on the menu.
- **Nobu Miami** – Co-owned by Robert DeNiro, this high-end sushi restaurant is one of the most popular dining spots on South Beach in Miami.
- **Wolfgang Puck Grand Café** – Located in Sunrise, FL, this restaurant is owned by the celebrity chef. Some of the most popular items on the menu include the Barbecued Duck Quesadilla, the Roasted Pumpkin Ravioli, and the Butternut Squash Soup.

Many Songs Have Been Written About Florida

Florida is the type of state that inspires songs. Miami, in particular, has been a source of inspiration for many musicians.

Here are some of the songs that were written about or mention Florida:

- "Designer Skyline" by Owl City
- "Florida" by Blue Rodeo
- "Florida" by Modest Mouse

- "Florida" by Patty Griffin
- "Florida" by Vic Chesnutt
- "Floridays" by Jimmy Buffett
- "Florida Blues" by Ricky Skaggs
- "Florida Rain" by Matt Bauer
- "Going Back to Miami" by Blues Brothers
- "Ice Ice Baby" by Vanilla Ice
- "Mainline Florida" by Eric Clapton
- "Miami" by Bob Seger
- "Miami" by Counting Crows
- "Miami" by U2
- "Miami" by Will Smith
- "Miami" by Randy Newman
- "Night Train" by James Brown
- "Only in Miami" by Bette Midler
- "State of Florida" by Less Than Jake
- "Turn the Lights Out When You Leave" by Elton John
- "Welcome to Dade County" by Pitbull

There's a Subgenre of Death Metal That Comes from Florida

In the 1980s, there was a lot of interest in death metal throughout Florida but in Tampa, especially—so much interest, in fact, that the city was recognized as the "Death Metal Capital of the World." Even to this day, death metal remains popular in the region.

There was a number of death metal bands that have

31

come out of Florida. Some of these include The Autumn Offering, The Absence, Cannibal Corpse, Death, Deicide, Diabolic, Malevolent Creation, Massacre, Monstrosity, Morbid Angel, Obituary, and Resurrection.

Death metal bands from Florida are categorized into the "Florida Death Metal" subgenre of music. Florida Death Metal isn't that well-defined, as there is a wide range of stylistic techniques used in the subgenre. Some Florida Death Metal consists of gory blood and guts themes, while some of it contains anti-Christian rants. The music is usually less technical, while vocals may range from grunts to trash yells and shrieks.

Morrisound Recording is a popular recording studio in Temple Terrace, Florida. This is where many of the Florida Death Metal bands have recorded their music.

You Can Visit Ernest Hemingway's House in Florida

Ernest Hemingway was one of the most influential American authors of all time. Did you know Hemingway and his wife lived in Key West, Florida from 1931 to 1939? Today, you can celebrate the author's legacy by visiting the Hemingway House, which is called the Ernest Hemingway Home & Museum.

At the museum, you'll get an inside glimpse at Ernest

Hemingway's life, including his writing desk and typewriter. The house is surrounded by gardens, which contain a lot of tropical plants.

The museum is also home to six-toed cats, all of which are descendants of Hemingway's original cats. While they are one of the museum's most popular attractions, the cats have also been at the center of some controversy over the years. The museum has been forced to tag the cats for identification purposes, but they continue to maintain a selective breeding program.

In 1988, the Hemingway House was featured in the movie *James Bond 007: Licence to Kill*. In the movie, James Bond is seen fleeing through the garden, while he's watched by guards across the street at the Key West lighthouse.

The Ritz Theatre Played a Role in African-American Pop Culture

The Ritz Theatre is located in the LaVilla neighborhood of Jacksonville. LaVilla has long been recognized as the "Harlem of the South." Between the 1920s and 1970s, LaVilla was considered a thriving neighborhood for African-American arts and culture. The neighborhood has been called a "mecca for African-American culture and heritage."

While it's Tennessee is credited with Blues music, the

actual term "The Blues" originated from a performance that took place in LaVilla in 1910.

Some of the most noteworthy musicians to ever perform at the Ritz Theatre during its early days included Ella Fitzgerald, Louis Armstrong, Duke Ellington, Cab Callaway, and Ray Charles.

While it remains a venue for live performances today, the Ritz Theatre is also home to the LaVilla Museum. The museum celebrates the theater's history and legacy as an African-American cultural icon and its role in the civil rights movement.

The Best-Selling Boy Band in History Was Formed in Florida

Did you know that the best-selling boy band in history was formed in Florida? With 130 million records sold worldwide, that band would the Backstreet Boys!

It all started out when Orlando natives AJ McLean and Howie Dorough met each other through auditions. They both later went on to meet Nick Carter at auditions. Realizing that they were able to harmonize together, the three of them decided to start a trio.

Kevin Richardson, who was from Lexington, Kentucky, moved to Orlando to work at Disney World. His co-worker introduced him to AJ McLean, Howie Dorough, and Nick Carter. As you can probably guess, he joined their group.

In 1992, Lou Pearlman posted an ad to form a vocal group in the *Orlando Sentinel*. AJ McLean auditioned in Pearlman's living room and was the first to be chosen for the band. After doing a lot of other auditions, Howie Dorough, Kevin Richardson, and Nick Carter were also chosen for the group. Kevin Richardson suggested his cousin, Brian Littrell. Littrell flew in from Kentucky to join the group as well—and ta-da! The most successful earning boy band in the history of all boy bands was born.

You might be surprised to learn that the name of the band actually came from Florida, too. Lou Pearlman named the band after an outdoor flea market in Orlando called Backstreet Market, which was popular among teenagers in the '90s.

The Backstreet Boys, who later came to be known as BSB, started to perform together throughout Florida. In fact, the band performed together for the very first time at SeaWorld Orlando in May of 1993. They later performed at a charity gala in Fort Lauderdale and other locations throughout Florida, including shopping malls and restaurants. They then traveled the country to perform at high schools to create a fanbase while they tried to score a record deal.

In 1994, the group got their signed to their first record label. Their debut album, *Backstreet Boys*, was released in 1995 and the rest is history. The group rose to fame with hit singles like "Quit Playin' Games (with My Heart),"

"I'll Never Break Your Heart," and "Anywhere for You."

It's hard to imagine what '90s music would have been like if the boys from the band hadn't met at those auditions!

A Famous Actor from Florida Was Almost Never an Actor at All

One famous actor who grew up in Florida was almost never an actor at all! Do you know who it is? Hint: he's most well-known for his roles in *What's Eating Gilbert Grape*, *Edward Scissorhands*, and *The Pirates of the Caribbean*. If you guessed Johnny Depp, then you guessed right.

While Johnny Depp was born in Owensboro, Kentucky, his family eventually moved to Miramar, Florida. While Depp was growing up in Florida, he aspired to be a musician and played the guitar in local garage bands, including The Kids and Rocky City Angels. Depp co-wrote the song "Mary" for the Rocky City Angels.

In 1983, Depp married Lori Anne Allison, who was the sister of the Rocky City Angels' bass player. Lori introduced Johnny Depp to actor Nicholas Cage. Cage talked Depp into becoming an actor.

Johnny Depp was cast in *A Nightmare on Elm Street* in 1984. The following year, Johnny Depp and his wife got divorced.

It's hard to imagine what the Hollywood movie industry would have been like if Johnny Depp had pursued his dream of being a musician instead. One thing's for sure: *The Pirates of the Caribbean* would have been lacking a great Jack Sparrow.

A Country/Pop Duo is Named After the Sunshine State

The country/pop duo Florida Georgia Line is (partially) named after Florida!

Brian Kelley grew up in Ormond Beach, Florida. He was a star pitcher on the high school baseball team and earned a scholarship to Florida State University. When Kelly realized he wouldn't be successful with the sport, he transferred to Belmont University in Nashville. It's there that he met Tyler Hubbard at a worship group.

After they graduated from Belmont University, Kelley and Hubbard gave themselves two years to see success as a country duo. They named themselves Florida Georgia Line after their home states. They were discovered by Joey Moi, Nickelback producer, at a county fair—and the rest is history!

Since then, the duo has released hit singles "Cruise," "Anything Goes," "This is How We Roll," "Dirt," and "H.O.L.Y."—just to name a few.

A Legendary Rock Singer Was from Florida

Did you know that one of the most legendary and influential rock stars of all time was born and raised in Florida?

Jim Morrison, who was the lead singer of the Doors, was born in Melbourne. While his family moved around, Morrison later returned to the state to live with his grandparents in Clearwater while he attended St. Petersburg College. He later transferred to Florida State University. He was arrested after he pulled a prank at a home football team.

While Jim Morrison was from Florida, the Doors wasn't formed in the state. It wasn't until Jim Morrison moved to Venice Beach in Los Angeles that he met Ray Manzarek, who he formed the Doors with. But to think it all started began in the Sunshine State!

Many Rock Bands Were Formed in Florida

While the Doors weren't formed in Florida, a lot of rock bands did originate from the Sunshine State!

Some of the most popular rock bands that were formed in Florida include:

- **Matchbox Twenty** – This band, featuring lead singer Rob Thomas, was formed in Orlando. Thomas, Brian Yale, and Paul Doucette were a part of the band Tabitha's Secret before breaking off to form their own band. Their first album, which featured "3 A.M." and "Push" helped them rise to fame.

- **Dashboard Confessional** – Formed in Boca Raton, this popular alternative rock/emo band features lead singer/songwriter Chris Carrabba. Carrabba was originally in the band Further Seems Forever, which was formed in Pompano Beach. Carrabba was recording his own music on the side. He released his LP, *The Swiss Army Romance*, under the name Dashboard Confessional. The band's name came from the song "The Sharp Hint of New Tears." When he released his second album, *The Places You Have Come to Fear the Most*, he left Further Seems Forever.

- **Shinedown** – This band was formed in Jacksonville by lead singer Brent Smith. Smith had a record deal with another band he was in previously. The record label dropped the band, however, and decided to keep only Smith. Thus, Shinedown was born. The band is most well-known for the song "Second Chance."

- **Tom Petty and the Heartbreakers** – This band was formed in Gainesville. The band's legendary frontrunner, Tom Petty, was also born and raised in Gainesville.

- **Creed** – The band Creed was formed in Tallahassee in the '90s. The band is most well-known for the songs "With Arms Wide Open," "Higher," and "My Sacrifice."

- **Cold** – Formed in Jacksonville in the late '80s, the band's most popular song is "Stupid Girl."

Florida is Known as "Hollywood East"

Of course, you know that Hollywood is the film capital of the world, but did you know that Florida has the nickname "Hollywood East"?

Film culture has been a part of Florida's history since the 1950s when *Follow That Dream*, a movie starring Elvis Presley was released. Since then, a number of productions have taken place in the state to capture its natural beauty, beaches, and cities.

The film industry has been a big source of revenue for the state. As of 2007, the Florida film industry was valued at more than $30 million.

Some of the most popular movies that have been filmed in Florida include:

- *2 Fast 2 Furious* – The second movie in the *Fast and the Furious* series was filmed in Boca Raton, West Palm Beach, and Hollywood, FL. Sylvester Stalone's Miami mansion is also featured in the film.
- *Ace Ventura: Pet Detective* – Starring Jim Carrey, this movie was filmed on location in Miami. Pro Player Stadium, otherwise known as Miami Dolphins Stadium, appears in the movie. The Villa Vizcaya mansion/museum is also featured in the film.

- *Caddyshack* – Scenes from this cult classic comedy starring Bill Murray were shot throughout Florida, which is no surprise since the movie is about golf and Florida is known for its many golf courses. Some of the places you can expect to see throughout the film include the Boca Raton Hotel, Biscayne Bay in Miami, Rolling Hills Golf Club (now Grande Oaks Golf Club) in Davie, and Plantation Country Club in Fort Lauderdale.
- *Edward Scissorhands* – The suburbs that are featured in this movie, which stars Johnny Depp and Winona Ryder, are located in Lakeland, Lutz, and the Tampa Bay area.
- *Marley & Me* – This tearjerker of a movie, starring Jennifer Aniston and Owen Wilson, was filmed throughout Florida. It features scenes in Miami, Fort Lauderdale, West Palm Beach, and Hollywood, FL.
- *Magic Mike* – This film, which stars Matthew McConaughey and Channing Tatum, is loosely based on Tatum's real-life story as a stripper in Tampa. The movie was filmed in Tampa, St. Petersburg, Ybor City, Tarpon Springs, and Tierra Verde.
- *My Girl* – Starring Macaulay Culkin, this beloved film was filmed in Mirror Lake, Sanford, Plant City, Ocoee, and Bartow, FL. The movie itself is set in Pennsylvania, however.

- *The Bodyguard* – Scenes from Whitney Houston's first movie were filmed in Miami. The Fontainebleau Hilton Resort is featured in the film.
- *The Water Boy* – While this movie takes place in Louisiana, it was filmed throughout Florida. EverBank Field in Jacksonville, the Citrus Bowl in Orlando, Stetson University, and Florida Southern College are all featured in the film.
- *Tomorrowland* – Scenes in this movie feature Smyrna Beach and the Carousel of Progress at Walt Disney World.
- *Transformers: Dark of the Moon* – This movie features scenes that take place at NASA's Kennedy Space Center.

A Famous Pop Singer/Actress Grew Up in Florida

Did you know singer/actress Mandy Moore grew up in Longwood, right outside of Orlando? Moore attended Bishop Moore Catholic High School in Orlando.

Mandy Moore began by singing the National Anthem at events throughout Orlando.

It was when Moore was working on her own demo at a recording studio in Orlando that she got her big break. A FedEx delivery man named Victor who had a friend at Epic Records just happened to overhear her singing. Victor gave his friend a copy of her demo, and Moore was given a recording deal with Epic Records.

Mandy Moore was only in the 9th grade when she signed with Epic. She had to leave her high school to record her debut album, but she was able to continue her education through tutors. By the summer of 1999, her first single, "Candy," had become a huge hit. Moore was compared to Britney Spears and Christina Aguilera, who were both popular at the time. The same year, Mandy Moore did two separate tours: one with NSYNC and another with the Backstreet Boys.

Moore later went on to have film success with small roles in movies like *Dr. Doolittle 2* and *The Princess Diaries*. Her real breakthrough as an actress came in 2002 when she starred alongside Shane West in *A Walk to Remember*, based on the Nicholas Sparks book of the same name.

Today, Mandy Moore stars in the hit TV show *This Is Us*. And we can thank Victor for spotting her at that Orlando recording studio!

A Soul Music Legend Started Out in Florida

Did you know that legendary blind musician Ray Charles was from Greenville, Florida? Charles attended the Florida School for the Deaf and the Blind in St. Augustine. It was there that he was taught to read braille music, which was a very difficult task.

While he was in high school, Charles performed on WFOY radio in St. Augustine.

After his mother died and he was expelled from school, Ray Charles began to play the piano at the Ritz Theatre. He worked at the theater for more than a year. He earned $4 a day, which was equal to about $50 today.

While he later set out for Seattle because he saw more opportunity to further his career, some of Charles' early recordings ("Wondering and Wondering," "I Found My Baby There," "Walking and Talking," and "Why Did You Go?") were recorded in the Sunshine State!

RANDOM FACTS

1. The first MTV spring break special was filmed at Daytona Beach in 1986. A performance from the Beastie Boys was featured in the special. It was also a historical moment in TV history: the term "woody" was used for the very first time.

2. Singer/actress Ariana Grande is from Boca Raton, Florida. While she was growing up, Grande went to Pine Crest School and North Broward Preparatory School. As a child, Grande performed at the Fort Lauderdale Children's Theater. She played the lead role in *Annie* and also starred in *Beauty and the Beast* and *The Wizard of Oz*. Her first television debut was when she sang "The Star-Spangled Banner" for the college football team, the Florida Panthers.

3. Gloria Estefan was born in Cuba but moved to Miami, Florida during her childhood. Estefan, who was raised Catholic, went to St. Michael-Archangel School and Our Lady of Lourdes Academy in Miami. She later went to the University of Miami. During that time, she worked as a translator for Miami International Airport. In 1975, she joined a Latino band called the Miami Sound Machine, which was started by Emilio Estefan, Jr. (Gloria's

now husband). The name was later changed to Gloria Estefan and the Miami Sound Machine before the singer eventually went on as a solo artist.

4. Actor Channing Tatum spent the majority of his teenage years in the Tampa area. Tatum rose to fame thanks to an audition in 2000 in Orlando, Florida. He was cast as a dancer in Ricky Martin's music video, "She Bangs." While Tatum only earned $400 for his performance, it led to his modeling career. He signed with Miami's Page 305 modeling agency. In 2006, Tatum starred in his breakthrough roles in the movies *She's the Man* alongside Amanda Bynes and *Step Up* with Jenna Dewan, who the actor later went on to marry.

5. Actor Ryan Gosling lived in Orlando, Florida while he was under contract for *The Mickey Mouse Club*. He wasn't asked to film as often as the other cast members because he wasn't thought to be as talented.

6. Model/actress Kate Upton grew up in Melbourne, Florida. She attended Holy Trinity Episcopal Academy. During her Florida upbringing, Upton was an equestrian who showed at the American Paint Horse Association and competed nationally. She won numerous equestrian awards, including four reserve championships. In 2008, she attended an Elite Model Management casting call and was

signed the very same day. By 2010, she had become the face of *Guess*.

7. The song "Beautiful Day in the Neighborhood" was written by Mr. Rogers as his senior thesis when he was attending Rollins College in Winter Park, Florida. If you take a boat tour in Winter Park, you can see the actor's lakefront home.

8. A number of TV shows have been set in Florida. Some of these include *Burn Notice*, *CSI: Miami*, *Dexter* (first season), *Empty Nest*, *Flipper*, *I Dream of Jeannie*, and *Miami Vice.*

9. Actor Burt Reynolds grew up in Riviera Beach, Florida. Reynolds attended Palm Beach High School and Florida State University where he won the Florida State Drama Award in 1956. The iconic actor later earned a star on the Hollywood Walk of Fame.

10. Actress Alexa Vega, who's most well-known for her role as Carmen Cortez in *Spy Kids*, was born in Miami. She lived in Ocala until she was four years old.

11. *Transformers* actress Megan Fox grew up in St. Petersburg, Florida where she trained in dance and drama. She later went onto win modeling awards in Hilton Head, South Carolina before making her big break in Hollywood.

12. Actress Bella Thorne grew up in Pembroke Pines, Florida. Her father, who was Cuban, died in an accident when she was 10 years old. This led Bella Thorne to become a serious child actress to help her struggling mom pay the bills. Thorne was bullied during her childhood because she was dyslexic and spoke Spanish while living in a suburban area.

13. *Twilight* actress Ashley Greene is from Jacksonville. Before she began her acting career, Greene attended University Christian School and Wolfson High School.

14. Born Tramar Dillard, the musician Flo Rida pays homage to his home state in his stage name. The singer/rapper is from Carol City, Florida.

15. *That '70s Show* actor Wilmer Valderrama was born in Miami. While his family moved back to Venezuela when he was three, they returned when he was 14.

16. The 1960s brought about a group called the Highwaymen. They were a group of African-American artists who painted Florida's beaches and coastal scenes using bold colors. They had a difficult time getting their paintings into a gallery, so the Highwaymen sold their paintings directly to motels, offices, etc. In the 21st century, their paintings sold for thousands of dollars. Michelle

Obama, Jeb Bush, and Steven Spielberg have purchased their paintings.

17. Arielle Kebbel was born in Winter Park, FL and attended the Crenshaw School in Winter Garden. Kebbel competed in the 2002 Miss Florida Teen USA beauty pageant. She was a full-time model before landing her role as Lindsay Lister in *The Gilmore Girls* when she moved to Los Angeles.

18. Actress Joanna Garcia, who's best known for her role as Cheyenne in *Reba*, grew up in Tampa. Her first performances were at a local theater. The actress was voted homecoming queen at Tampa Catholic High School. While she was in high school, she starred in three seasons of the Nickelodeon show, *Are You Afraid of the Dark?* Garcia made the commute from Florida to Montreal to film the show.

19. Former *Saturday Night Live* comedian Darrell Hammond grew up in Melbourne, Florida. At one point, he worked as a voiceover artist in Orlando.

20. Fred Durst, head vocalist of the band Limp Bizkit, grew up in Jacksonville. After he left the Navy after two years, he moved back to Jacksonville where he worked on forming Limp Bizkit. At the time, he also worked in landscaping and as a tattoo artist. When the band Korn performed in the area, Durst invited them back to his house and

convinced them to listen to Limp Bizkit's demo. Korn liked what they heard and added Limp Bizkit as an opening act to their tour. The rest is history!

Test Yourself – Questions and Answers

1. Which legendary musician's first indoor concert was held at the Florida Theater?
    a. Charles Ray
    b. Elvis Presley
    c. Jim Morrison

2. The Backstreet Boys were named after Backstreet Market, which is a _____.
    a. An outdoor flea market in Orlando
    b. A fish market in Orlando
    c. A grocery store in Orlando

3. Which famous author's house is now a museum you can visit in Florida?
    a. Dr. Seuss
    b. Stephen King
    c. Ernest Hemingway

4. Mandy Moore was discovered in Florida when her singing was overheard by:
    a. Lou Pearlman, creator of the Backstreet Boys
    b. A FedEx deliverer named Victor who had a friend at Epic Records
    c. Charles Ray

5. Ariana Grande's first performance at the Fort Lauderdale Children's Theater was as:
    a. Belle in *Beauty and the Beast*
    b. Dorothy in *Wizard of Oz*
    c. Annie in *Annie*

Answers

1. b.
2. a.
3. c.
4. b.
5. c.

CHAPTER THREE

FACTS ABOUT FLORIDA'S ATTRACTIONS

If you're thinking about visiting Florida, you probably know that it's full of attractions. The most famous is, of course, Walt Disney World Resort in Orlando. It draws in an estimated 46 million visitors each year, making it the world's most popular resort. But what do you really know about the theme park? Do you know why—or how—Walt Disney kept the plan to build the park a secret? Do you know what's special about LEGOLAND? Do you know what the state's oldest attraction is? Do you know what surprising animals can both be found in the state and where they can be found? Do you know what Wiki Wachee is most famous for? Do you know what nationally televised event is held in the state? Read on to learn more about the many things to do and see in the Sunshine State!

Disney World's Beginnings Were Kept a Secret

Today, Disney World is home to Magic Kingdom,

Epcot, Hollywood Studios, Animal Kingdom parks, along with Typhoon Lagoon and Blizzard Beach water parks. But do you know how it all began?

Walt Disney first built Disneyland in Anaheim, California, but he soon realized that he needed to expand. A lot of businesses began to open near Disneyland. He wanted more control, which required him to acquire more land. Noticing that only 5% of the park's visitors were coming from the east, which is where 3/4 Americans lived at the time, he knew that it was in his best interest to open a park on the east coast.

Walt Disney decided to acquire the land in secret, however. He was afraid that people would realize he was the one who was acquiring land, which might lead other businesses to buy up the area like they had in California. To prevent this from happening, he used fake corporations to purchase 30,500 acres of land. Even the real estate agents didn't know his true identity, and he didn't sign any paperwork until he had secured all the property.

People began to make speculations about who was acquiring the land. Many assumed that NASA was developing their Kennedy Space Center. Others believed Ford, Howard Hughes or the Rockefellers were the ones purchasing the land.

The *Orlando Sentinel* was the first to crack the mystery after one reporter interviewed Walt Disney and caught him off-guard. They published an article titled "We Say 'Mystery Industry' is Disney." Although Disney originally denied the reporter's claims during the interview, he asked Florida Governor Haydon Burns to confirm the story's accuracy after it was published.

Walt Disney World's Magic Kingdom is on the Second Floor

When you visit the Magic Kingdom theme park at Walt Disney World, you might think you're standing at ground level… but actually, you're not.

One of Disney's not-so-best kept secrets is that there are "underground" tunnels beneath Magic Kingdom. Technically, it's not *actually* underground but on the ground floor. Florida is too swampy for the tunnels to actually be underground. But tell that to guests, who believe they're at ground level.

The underground system, which is known as the "Utilidors," was designed for employees and maintenance to travel beneath the park without guests noticing. Walt Disney allegedly thought seeing a staff member walking to his post was "jarring," which was what led to the idea. It's also a place where Mickey and Minnie go to get out of their costumes and cool off.

The tunnels encompass nine acres and offer a number of accommodations for employees, such as dressing rooms, cafeterias, a hair salon, makeup rooms, and more. Since the underground tunnel system is so large, employees sometimes ride golf carts down there to get around.

To get to the tunnels, employees also have to walk underneath the lake the ferry takes guests over to get to Main Street Station.

So, next time you're at Magic Kingdom, just remember that someone might be eating their lunch or hanging out beneath you!

The Florida Everglades is Home to Both Alligators and Crocodiles

This might not sound like such a big deal, but did you know the Florida Everglades is the only place on the entire planet where you'll find both alligators *and* crocodiles?

Both alligators and crocodiles can both be found in the state, but alligators greatly outnumber crocodiles. It's been estimated that there are 500 to 1,200 crocodiles in Florida, while there's believed to be anywhere from 1.3 to 2 million alligators in Florida. This means that there's approximately one alligator for every 10 to 15 people who call the Sunshine State home.

It's actually a pretty big deal that so many alligators and crocodiles can be found in Florida since they were both once endangered in the state. Thanks to Florida's conservation efforts, alligators are no longer endangered, while crocodiles' endangerment status in the state has been changed to "threatened," according to the National Park Service. Crocodiles remain endangered throughout the rest of the world.

Fun fact: The alligator is also the Florida state animal. Chose in 1987, the reptile was selected as a representation of Florida's untamed swamps and wilderness.

You Can See Mermaids—and Receive Mermaid Lessons—in Wiki Wachee

The most famous mermaids in the entire country can be found at Wiki Wachee Springs State Park!

You can see a mermaid show at the underwater theater just about every day at the park. Mermaids perform *The Little* Mermaid. The performance includes musical numbers. The mermaids will also perform a number of underwater stunts that might surprise you, such as eating and drinking.

If you or your little one has any interest in mermaid training, then Wiki Wachee is just the place for you! The park offers mermaid camps, one for children between the ages of 7-14 and one for adults over the age of 30. Campers will get to experience what it takes to be a mermaid at Wiki Wachee Springs State Park and will receive training in underwater ballet.

Before attending camp, you must first get SCUBA, CPR, and first aid certified, as well as have a few months of training to breathe through a hose. That being said, adult campers will get a certificate of completion and children will have a chance to be a dry performer in *The Little Mermaid* once they've completed the weekend-long camp.

There's a Secret Parade for Guests Who Arrive Early at SeaWorld Orlando

SeaWorld Orlando is known for its shows, animal encounters, and rides. But did you know there's also a secret parade for guests who arrive early to the park?

If you arrive at the park early and head towards the Manta roller coaster, you'll see a "flamingo parade"! The flamingos are accompanied by SeaWorld Orlando employees, who lead them from the enclosure to live in to the flamingo exhibit.

While the flamingo parade doesn't last long, it's a great opportunity to get some amazing photos of the flamingos!

Many Bird Species Can Be Found at Dry Tortugas National Park

Did you know that more species of birds can be found at Dry Tortugas National Park than turtles? This might not be *too* surprising—until you learn about how the park got its name.

When Juan Ponce de Leon visited the area, he named it "Tortugas," the Spanish word that means "turtle or tortoise." He chose the name due to the high number of turtles he found in the area. (The reason "dry" is in the national park's name has to do with the island's lack of fresh water on its surface).

Dry Tortugas National Park is a popular nesting spot for sea turtles. Three different species of sea turtles (green turtles, hawksbill turtles, and loggerhead turtles) can all be found at the park.

The park is also home to over 300 bird species. A few of these species don't nest anywhere else in the entire country, including the masked booby, the sooty tern, the magnificent frignate bird, and the brown noddy.

It's surprising the park, which gets about 80,000 visitors a year, wasn't named after birds.

Only One of Universal Studios Florida's Original Attractions is Still Open Today

Did you know that most of the original attractions that were there on Universal Studios' opening day in 1990 have since closed?

Diagon Alley, an attraction at the Wizarding World of Harry Potter, is now located at the original Jaws attraction.

Earthquake will be replaced with Fast & Furious: Supercharged in the near future.

In 2004, Revenge of the Mummy: The Ride replaced Kongfrontation.

So, which attraction remains? The E.T. Adventure, which is based on the movie *E.T., the Extra-Terrestrial.*

The Diving Capital of the World is in Florida

Did you know the "Diving Capital of the World" can be found in the Sunshine State? Key Largo, which is the most northern of the Florida Keys, has earned this title. The city attracts thousands of scuba divers every year and for good reason! Key Largo is home to not only the only coral reef in the United States but the third largest coral reef *in the entire world!*

At 160 miles long, the Florida Reef is only smaller than the Great Barrier Reef in Australia and the Belize Barrier Reef. The Florida Reef is preserved through the Florida Keys National Marine Sanctuary.

Key Largo is also a popular vacation spot for sports fishers. It's home to the Fantastic II, which is the most famous sports fishing center in the whole world.

And that's not all! There are plenty of other things to see and do in Key Largo. It's home to John Pennekamp Coral Reef State Park, the only underwater state park in the country, and Dagny Johnson Key Largo Hammock Botanical State Park.

Filmmakers have been drawn to the area, which is no surprise due to its botanical beauty. Key Largo holds an annual Humphrey Bogart Film Festival, which is the only film festival in the country that honors the movie legend. Key Largo also hosts Fantasy Fest every year.

You Can Swim with Dolphins in Florida

If swimming with dolphins is on your bucket list, then look no further than the Sunshine State. There are a number of places where you can swim with dolphins. Some of the most popular places include:

- **Discovery Cove** – Perhaps the most well-known place to swim with dolphins in Florida, this theme park has everything for aquatic lovers. You can also feed tropical birds, interact with otters and marmosets, go snorkeling, lounge in the pools, and more. Discovery Cove is one of Orlando's top attractions.
- **Dolphin Research Center** – With its location in Grassy Key, FL, the Dolphin Research Center rehabilitates and provides a safe environment for rescued dolphins. Since part of its mission is to help humans to better interact with dolphins, it offers encounters and the opportunity to swim with dolphins. It's also the only place in Florida that's licensed to rescue manatees.
- **Gulf World Marine Park** – Located in Panama

City Beach, this park offers you a chance to swim with the dolphins and have close encounters with other marine life, including harbor seals, stingrays, and sea lions.

- **Miami Seaquarium** – The Seaquarium provides you with the chance to swim with the dolphins, take a dolphin ride, and have other close-up encounters with the dolphins.

You Can Taste Gator at Gatorland... If You Dare

When you visit Gatorland, which is one of Orlando's oldest attractions, you'll find plenty of unique experiences. The park is home to more than 2,000 alligators, including the largest collection of white leucistic alligators. You'll also find crocodiles, Florida panthers, Florida bobcats, and other animals. But did you know you can also taste gator when you're at Gatorland?

The park's eatery, Pearl's Good Eats, serves Gator Nuggets, which are fried pieces of alligator meat. This may sound like a crazy or strange concept, but gator meat is actually quite popular among Floridians. The Gatorland website assures us that gator nuggets are *not* made from the park's alligators.

Don't worry, though. The park offers a number of other menu items, including hot dogs, hamburgers, chicken tenders, peanut butter and jelly, and more, so there are plenty of other options if you choose not to try out some gator meat.

Coral Castle is One of Florida's Greatest Mysteries and Most Interesting Attractions

You may have heard of Coral Castle in Miami, but do you know the story behind it or why it's one of Florida's greatest mysteries?

The story goes like this: Edward Leedskalnin from Latvia was engaged to marry his sweetheart, Agnes Scuffs. Sadly, she called off the wedding the day before it was about to take place.

Ed made it his mission to build a monument for his lost love. With no help from anyone else, he allegedly built the Coral Castle. Between the years of 1923 to 1951, he sculpted and carved more than 1,100 tons of coral rock.

Many people don't believe that Ed, who was just five-feet tall and weighed 100 pounds, could have done it alone. Coral could be up to 4,000 feet thick. While he allegedly was skilled from working in lumber camps when he lived in Latvia, some have bounced around the theory that he might have had supernatural powers. When he was alive, Ed used to say he knew the secrets that were used to build Egypt's ancient pyramids, making people wonder even more if he might have had secret powers. Even more curiously, no one ever saw him working on the stone structure.

Regardless of how it was built, you can visit the Coral Castle Museum today and take a tour of Ed's creation.

LEGOLAND Contains a Piece of Florida's Theme Park History

When you visit LEGOLAND Florida, there's no doubt that you expect to see the brick sculptures, rides, and other attractions the theme park has to offer. But did you know LEGOLAND also contains a piece of Florida's theme park history?

The theme park was built on the site that was once Cypress Gardens. As you might remember from chapter one, Cypress Gardens was the first theme park to *ever* open in Florida.

Rather than completely eliminate any trace that Cypress Gardens ever existed, LEGOLAND chose to incorporate a couple of small parts of the park into its design. There's a vintage gazebo and a banyan tree that's more than 80 years old that remains in the park today. LEGOLAND also contains some of the original park's beautiful botanicals. Not only does this provide park visitors with a cool place to catch some shade, but it also takes you to an entirely different world while you're in LEGOLAND.

The Country's Only Seashell Museum Can Be Found in Florida

The Bailey-Matthews National Shell Museum is the only museum in all of America that's dedicated to shells. The museum features 30 permanent exhibits containing shells from not just Florida but the entire world!

One of the museum's exhibits is the "Shells of Sanibel & Captiva." The exhibit has some of the most beautiful shells from the region on display. Museum visitors will also learn more information on how to find shells in the region, as well as how to clean them. It's a useful exhibit for anyone who plans to search for shells in the area.

Some of the other permanent exhibits at the Bailey-Matthews National Shell Museum include "Shells from Around the World," "Record Breaking Sized Shells," "Sailors' Valentines," "Shells in Architecture, Art, and Human History," and "Cameos, Shell Inlay, Buttons, and Bows."

Bayfront Park Hosts a Televised Celebration Each Year

Did you know that Bayfront Park is home to Miami's New Year's Eve celebration each year?

The nationally-televised celebration is hosted by musician and Miami native Pitbull each year. It's called "Pitbull's New Year's Revolution."

Rather than watching a ball drop, Miamians get to see the "Big Orange" rise at midnight. There's also a firework display when the clock hits midnight.

The show is free for anyone to attend and best of all? Partygoers don't need to battle with frigid temperatures the way New Yorkers do when they go to watch the ball drop, which Pitbull admits is why he started hosting the event rather than performing at Dick Clark's Rockin' Eve celebration, despite disappointing fans. Who can blame him? Miami temperatures tend to range between 60 and 70 degrees for the celebration. What a way to ring in the New Year.

You Can Ride a Glass Bottom Boat in Florida

Recognized as Florida's "oldest attraction," the Glass Bottom Boats at Silver Springs State Park is one of the best ways to get a glimpse of some of the river's beauty. You'll float on a boat with a clear glass bottom to view the underwater life.

During the boat tour, you'll also get a chance to see some of Silver Springs' history, including a Native American row boat and Hollywood movie props.

RANDOM FACTS

1. Walt Disney World's Aquarium of the Seas at Epcot is the second largest aquarium in the country! With 5.7 million gallons of water, the only aquarium larger is the Georgia Aquarium.

2. Everglades National Park is the 3rd largest national park in the entire country. The park, which encompasses 1.5 million acres, attracts an annual one million or more visitors each year.

3. Miami is the only city in the country that's bordered by two national parks: Everglades National Park and Biscayne National Park. The city is also home to 800 parks of its own.

4. The Florida Museum of Hispanic and Latin American Art is the only museum in the country that's dedicated to preserving artwork by Hispanic and Latin American artists. The museum is located in Coral Gables, Florida.

5. It's been estimated that there are more than 375,000 hotel rooms throughout the state of Florida. Of those, more than 30,000 are located at Walt Disney World resorts.

6. One Florida beach town has been nicknamed the "Shark Tooth Capital of the World." Beachgoers

have been finding prehistoric shark teeth in Venice, Florida for years. The reason shark teeth are so common in the area is that Florida was submerged underwater 10 million years ago. Although no dinosaur fossils have been discovered in the state, shark tooth hunters have found many fossilized teeth over rock formations from prehistoric shark species, including the megalodon shark in Venice Beach.

7. The Sunshine State is one of the best places to go if you love the beach. Regardless of what part of Florida you visit, you'll never be more than 60 miles away from the ocean!

8. Since the 1920s, Daytona Beach has been referred to as the "World's Most Famous Beach." It gained its popularity due to its automobile testing and racing.

9. Florida's Annual Mug Race, which starts in Palatka and ends in Jacksonville, is the longest sailboat race in the world. It's been taking place every year since 1954.

10. Florida is home to a Native American reservation. Big Cypress Reservation, which is located in the Everglades, is home to the Seminole Tribe of Florida. The reservation offers a tour of the Seminole Tribe's culture, The Ah-Tah-Thi-Ki Museum is home to 30,000 artifacts. There's also a

boardwalk that leads to the village the tribe lives in where you'll find Seminole natives creating baskets and jewelry. There's also a campground you can stay at to learn more about their lifestyle.

11. There are only two round freshwater lakes in the world and Florida is home to one of them. Lake DeFuniak is believed to have been formed due to a sinkhole, though legends say the lake is the result of a meteor.

12. Crystal River and Three Sisters Springs offer lots of opportunities to spot some of Florida's wildlife. The region is famous for its manatees, mainly because it's the only place in the United States where it's legal to swim with them!

13. The deepest natural spring in America can be found in Florida! Located in Weeki Wachee, cave divers can enter the cave at the spring. The Weeki Wachee Spring has an average depth of 265 feet.

14. The world's largest McDonald's is located in Orlando. It's nothing like any other McDonald's you've ever been to. The fast-food restaurant serves custom brick-oven pizza, pasta, sandwiches, omelets, Belgian waffles, and treats from its desserts bar!

15. The Presidents Hall of Fame, which is located in Clermont, is a one of its kind museum that's dedicated to preserving the history of the presidents

of the United States. Its exhibits include a White House mini replica, authentic First Ladies' Inaugural Gowns, a mini replica of Mount Rushmore, an animatronic Franklin D. Roosevelt, and more.

16. Myakka Canopy Walkway in Sarasota is the only city on the planet where you can observe a subtropical forest from the treetops. The 85-foot boardwalk is built more than 20 feet above the ground, which can make for great wildlife and bird-watching.

17. The largest man-made reef in the world is located near Key Biscayne. The Neptune Memorial Reef encompasses 16 acres of the ocean floor. Not only is the reef a hotspot among scuba divers and marine biologists, but it's also a very popular spot for people to spread the ashes of their loved ones. Another place in Florida where ashes are commonly spread (even though it's illegal)? Walt Disney World!

18. Morikami Museum and Japanese Gardens in Delray Beach is a mecca for Japanese culture in Florida. With exhibits, monthly tea ceremonies, and traditional Japanese festivals throughout the year, you can learn a lot about the culture of Japan.

19. You can go on a drive-through safari in Florida. Located in Loxahatchee, Lion Country Safari features more than 1,000 animals.

20. The Fort Lauderdale Antique Car Museum features cars dating back to 1900! The museum, which takes up 30,000 square feet, has the largest collection of Packard cars in the country.

Test Yourself – Questions and Answers

1. Where can you find both wild alligators and crocodiles?

   a. The Florida Keys
   b. Daytona Beach
   c. The Florida Everglades

2. Where can you attend mermaid training camp in Florida?

   a. Wiki Wachee
   b. Miami
   c. Daytona Beach

3. The world's largest McDonald's is located in which of the following Florida cities?

   a. Miami
   b. Orlando
   c. Jacksonville

4. The first theme park in Florida was _____.

   a. Cypress Gardens
   b. Walt Disney World
   c. Gatorland

5. What is the "oldest attraction" in Florida?

   a. The Presidents Hall of Fame
   b. The Bailey-Matthews National Shell Museum
   c. The Glass Bottom Boats at Silver Springs State Park

Answers

1. c.
2. a.
3. b.
4. a.
5. c.

CHAPTER FOUR

FLORIDA'S INVENTIONS, IDEAS, AND MORE!

Have you ever wondered what inventions have come out of Florida? A number of popular products, foods, and businesses have originated from the Sunshine State. Do you know which type of pie or what type of sandwich the state is famous for? Do you know about the college professor who invented a popular sports drink? Do you know what inventions out of Florida are currently in the works? Here, we'll take a closer look at some of the things from your daily life that originated from Florida!

Burger King

Today, it's one of the most famous fast food chains in the country and world famous for its Whopper sandwich. Did you know Burger King got its start in Florida? And it didn't start out as "Burger King," either. The first restaurant, which opened in 1953 in Jacksonville, was originally called Insta-Burger King.

After visiting the first McDonald's store in San Bernardino, California, the co-founders (Keith J. Kramer and his uncle-in-law, Matthew Burns) purchased the rights to an "Insta-Broiler." The machine, which was used to produce as much food as quickly as possible, turned out to be so efficient that Kramer and Burns had them installed in all of the Insta-Burger King franchises.

Insta-Burger King saw a few years of success, but by 1959, the company began to fail under their ownership. It was purchased by Jams McLamore and David R. Edgerton, who co-owned the Miami franchise. They restructured the chain and were the ones who changed its name to Burger King. McLamore and Edgerton expanded the franchise to 250 more locations before selling the corporation to the Pillsbury Company in the late 1960s. It would go on to switch ownership several more times over the years.

As of 2016, there were more than 15,500 stores in 100 different countries, including Australia's Hungry Jack's.

Key Lime Pie

Key lime pie is a favorite among many Americans. You can find it at just about any diner, bakery or you might even have a beloved recipe of your own. But did you know it came from Florida? Key West, to be exact. That's where the "key" in key lime comes from.

Who invented the recipe? Well, no one seems to know for sure, but there are several possible theories.

Some say that Jack Simons, a botanist, is responsible for inventing the first key lime pie recipe. There's no information out there to potentially back up this theory, however, so it seems like the least likely one.

The first official mention of a key lime pie recipe came from William Curry, the first millionaire of Key West and a ship salvager. He wrote in a journal that his cook, someone who he called Aunt Sally, allegedly made him a key lime pie. But there are a lot of skeptics of this theory, too. It's believed that *if* Aunt Sally really did make a key lime pie for Curry, she probably wasn't the inventor of the recipe. Who did it invent it? The local sponge fishermen seem like the most likely culprits.

The sponge fishermen would go out on their boats for days at a time, which meant they were always looking for ways to store non-perishable foods. Well, the ingredients of the original key lime pie recipe (condensed milk, limes, and eggs) are, in fact, non-perishable food items. The recipe also didn't call for cooking, either, making it perfect for fishermen.

Regardless of who invented it, Floridians take their key lime pie pretty seriously. Back in 1965, a Florida state representative actually tried to fine people who advertised key lime pie that wasn't made with actual key limes. That didn't pass, but in 1994, the Florida State Legislature recognized key lime pie as the official state pie.

Coppertone Sunscreen

Have you ever wondered who to thank when you lather your skin up with sunscreen at the pool or the beach?

The very first sunscreen was invented by Benjamin Green, a pharmacist from Miami, in 1944.

In addition to being a pharmacist, Green also served as an airman in World War II. When the world learned about the risks associated with sun exposure, Green wanted to design a product that would protect soldiers' skin. What he really wanted was to protect his own son when he went to serve in the war.

Green used red veterinary petroleum, or "red vet pet", which was supposed to act as a physical barrier between the sun and skin. Unfortunately, his earliest sunscreen formula didn't go over so well. *The New York Times* called the sunscreen "heavy and unpleasant." It had a sticky texture, it was red in color, and it also wasn't very effective. No one really wanted to use it.

Once World War II ended, Green experimented some more and changed the formula. He added cocoa butter and coconut oil to the red vet pet. The product was more pleasant and was a bigger hit this time around. Green named his product Coppertone.

In 1956, the Coppertone logo—a girl and her dog on the beach—that we all recognize today was first introduced.

We can't thank for Benjamin Green for the invention of SPF, however. He's only responsible for creating a barrier method of sunscreen. SPF wasn't introduced until 1962 by Franz Geiter, a Swiss who also began to work on a sunscreen of his own in the 1940s after experiencing a bad sunburn.

Modern Refrigeration and Air Conditioning Technology

It might not surprise you to learn that refrigeration was developed in Florida. What might surprise you, however, is *why* it was invented. Shockingly, it wasn't just to keep things cool. It was to save lives.

A physician in Florida named Dr. John Gorrie is known today as the "father of air conditioning" and the "father of refrigeration." He invented the technology that would lead to the world's first refrigerator in 1841 when there was a Yellow Fever outbreak in Apalachicola. Gorrie really believed that cold was the key to treating illness. He introduced the idea of using ice to help reduce fevers among sick patients. Ice was received in the form of boat shipments from northern lakes while Dr. Gorrie experimented—quite successfully—with gas expansion in order to refrigerate.

While his invention never became famous or was properly funded prior to his death, there are several monuments and a museum in his honor in Apalachicola today.

Gorrie's experiments and findings in refrigeration are considered to play a key role in air conditioning as well.

It's hard to imagine what summer would be like without this Floridian's idea!

Gatorade

Today, you'll find Gatorade at just about any theme park, sporting event or maybe even in your own fridge. While it's only recommended to athletes and people who are suffering from dehydration, most of us have drunk it at some point during our lifetimes. But did you know the drink got its start in Florida? In fact, Gatorade is actually named after the Florida Gators. You might have known this already, but do you know why or how the sports drink came about?

Back in 1965, an assistant football coach at the University of Florida noticed his players were being affected by the heat. He approached Dr. Robert Cade, a medicine and nephrology professor at the university, to find out why the players weren't urinating after their games.

Dr. Cade and his team of researchers quickly discovered that the players were losing electrolytes through their sweat and not being replaced. Cade and his researchers developed the rehydration drink, but they weren't a hit early on. In fact, the earliest versions of the drink tasted so bad that they made the players vomit. They allegedly tasted like saltwater. The flavor improved when Dr. Cade's wife, Mary, suggested adding lemon juice to the drink.

Gatorade proved to be successful for the team. The players were given the drink, which led to the Florida Gators winning the Orange Bowl for the first time in history in 1967.

The same year, Dr. Cade sold the rights to his drink to Stokely-Van Camp, a company which had only been known previously for its pork and beans. The rest is history. Gatorade's lightning bolt logo was born in 1973 and the drink is popular in many different flavor options throughout the country today.

The Melting Pot

You've probably heard of the Melting Pot, the popular fondue restaurant chain. Did you know that the Melting Pot got started in the Sunshine State?

The first restaurant was opened in Maitland, Florida, which is located near Orlando. You might be surprised to learn that the original Melting Pot menu was nowhere near as big as it is today. In fact, it only offered three items: beef fondue and Swiss cheese fondue, as well as a milk chocolate fondue that was served for dessert.

Mark Johnston, who was a waiter at the restaurant, recognized its potential. He and his brothers, Mike and Bob, got permission from the owners to start their own Melting Pot restaurant in Tallahassee, which they opened in 1979. Their restaurant became a huge success and they began to expand the menu.

By 1981, they had opened a second location of their own in Tampa. By the mid-1980s, the Johnson brothers had acquired all rights to the Melting Pot brand.

Sadly, you can no longer visit the original Melting Pot restaurant in Maitland, as it was shut down in 2008. However, the chain can be found throughout the rest of the country and even in Canada!

Rum Runner

Whether you've tried one or not, you've probably heard of a mixed drink called the Rum Runner. Did you know this popular cocktail originated from Florida?

The tropical drink originated from the Florida Keys. The drink came about in the late 1950s and came from the Holiday Isle Tiki Bar in Islamorada, Florida. The bar allegedly had to get rid of some of its rum and liquors before they could receive a new shipment of inventory, so the hotel manager dared the bartender to come up with a drink that would use the excess alcohol.

The bartender came up with a concoction containing banana liqueur, blackberry liqueur, rum, brandy, grenadine, orange juice, and pineapple juice. The drink turned out to be a hit, which is popular among Florida spring breakers today!

IBM Personal Computer and the Term "PC"

Did you know you can thank Florida for your personal computer? The IBM Personal Computer came from the Sunshine State.

The personal computer was designed by a team at IBM's Boca Raton division. Designed Don Estridge led the team to create the IBM 5150. It was first released to the public market in August of 1981.

While people used the term "personal computer" prior to the release of IBM thanks to Xerox's PARC's Alto, it was the IBM Personal Computer that really popularized "PC." In fact, the entire meaning of the term changed, as it came to mean a desktop microcomputer that was IBM compatible.

The Cuban Sandwich

You've probably heard of or may have even tried a Cuban sandwich, but do you know where the sandwich originated from?

No one knows for sure if the Cuban sandwich was brought to Florida by Cuban immigrants or if it was first invented in Florida. Signs point to it being invented in Florida, however.

The first documented Cuban sandwich was in 1900 when it was served at cafeterias in Ybor City and West Tampa. A lot of Cuban immigrants were working at the cigar factories in the areas at the time and the Cuban sandwich was served to them in the cafeterias. Since this is the first record of the Cuban sandwich, many believe it was, in fact, invented in Florida.

The sandwich is said to be one of Tampa's signature foods.

The popularity of the sandwich quickly caught on. It became a popular menu item in Miami by the 1960s. A lot of Cubans immigrated to the area, which is why it likely became so popular.

The sandwich has since gained popularity in cities with Cuban communities, such as New York City and Chicago, as well as cities throughout New Jersey.

A Cuban sandwich consists of glazed ham, roast pork, Swiss cheese, dill pickles, and mustard on Cuban bread.

Frozen Condensed Orange Juice and Tropicana Orange Juice

Did you know that frozen condensed orange juice was invented in Florida? It was created by the University of Florida's Citrus Research and Education Center. They came up with the idea in the 1940s to provide juice to soldiers, but frozen condensed orange juice became popular with the general population as well.

It's also probably no surprise to you that Tropicana started out in Florida. But how much do you really know about the company's origins?

It all started out with an Italian immigrant named Anthony T. Rossi. He came to the United States when he was 21 years old. By 1947, he began farming in Palmetto, Florida. He opened a company called Manatee River Packing Company, where he began to pack fruit gift boxes and jars of fruit for salads.

Over time, the company began to grow and relocated to Bradenton, Florida. Rossi changed the name of his business to Fruit Industries. His company supplied some of the fruits for the fruit salads at the Waldorf-Astoria Hotel in New York.

Rossi also began to produce frozen concentrate orange juice at this time.

By the early 1950s, Rossi had purchased the Grapefruit Canning Company in Bradenton and began to produce orange juice. When the orange juice saw a lot of success, Rossi stopped producing fruit boxes.

Rossi is responsible for the flash pasteurization process, which he created in 1954. The process preserves the juice's taste by increasing its temperature for a short time. This allowed customers to get a fresh taste of pure not-from-concentrate juice in a package… or, in other words, Tropicana Pure Premium.

The company created a cartoon logo for the juice, which was called Tropic-Ana. The cartoon mascot was a girl wearing a Hawaiian grass skirt and lei and carrying oranges on her head. The company got rid of the logo in the 1980s, however.

Today, Tropicana is the largest buyer of fruit in Florida. The company gets its fruit from over 400 Florida groves. While it used Brazilian oranges for a brief time in 2007 due to hurricanes that damaged Florida's supply, the company returned to only using oranges from the Sunshine State in 2012.

Red Lobster

Today, it's most well-known for its famous Lobster Fest and Endless Shrimp promotions, but did you know the Red Lobster chain start out in Florida?

The very first Red Lobster was opened in 1968 in Lakeland, Florida. It was opened by Bill Darden, who had a dream: to provide affordable, high-quality seafood meals to people from all areas of the country.

Just two years later, General Mills took notice of Red Lobster. General Mills decided to back the company, and the franchise began to rapidly expand throughout the country during the 1980s.

In 1974, Red Lobster released its popcorn shrimp, which was a huge draw among customers. But the menu item that developed a real cult following in 1992 when the chain introduced its Cheddar Bay Biscuits.

By 2016, Red Lobster became a world leader in seafood. The chain has more than 700 locations and can be found in 11 different countries. Its legendary Cheddar Bay Biscuits can even be found in the frozen section at most grocery stores.

And to think it all started out in Lakeland, Florida!

Th Home Shopping Network

The Home Shopping Network is one of the easiest ways to shop from your own home. It's easy, convenient, and a nightmare for shopping addicts. Did you know that the HSN started out in Florida?

Originally called the Home Shopping Club, the network was founded by Lowell "Bud" Paxson and Roy Speer back in 1982.

The idea came about due to a radio station Paxson was managing. One of the advertisers was having liquidity problems, which led them to pay the station in the form of can openers. The station was in need of money, so a radio personality from the station went on the radio and sold them for $9.95 a piece. He was able to make the can openers completely sell out.

That radio personality was Bob Circosta, who became Home Shopping Club's first home shopping host. During the course of his position with the network, he sold more than 70,000 products.

The network was first only seen by residents of Pinellas County, Florida, who could watch it through their local cable networks.

Three years later, in 1985, it became the first home shopping network in the country. The same year, the network's name was changed to Home Shopping Network. In 1986, it saw its first competitor, QVC.

After the co-founders of HSN passed away in 2012 and 2015 and the HSN CEO left the company for Weight Watchers, HSN was acquired by QVC.

Black Diamond Guitar Strings

Just about every musician has heard of the Black Diamond Guitar Strings brand. Did you know the company started out in the Sunshine State?

Based in Sarasota, Florida, the brand, which claims to

be a "small" custom shop, is known to make some of the highest quality guitar strings on the market today. It provides acoustic strings, electric strings, bass strings, and guitar-related accessories, such as picks and straps.

A number of famous musicians have used Black Diamond Guitar Strings. Some of the most well-known artists who have used the brand include Bret Michaels, Caroline Kole, and Josh Turner.

Publix

You've probably heard of the Publix chain of supermarkets, even if you've never actually been to one. Did you know the chain started out in the Sunshine State?

The first Publix market was opened by George Jenkins in 1930. Four years later, that store made $120,000—the equivalent of more than $2 million today.

In 1935, Jenkins opened a second market, which he called the Economy Food Store, in Winter Haven. Even during the Great Depression, both markets saw financial success.

By 1940, Jenkins purchased an orange grove, on which he built his first actual supermarket. The store had air conditioning, cold and refrigerated foods, an in-store donut shop, an in-store floral shop, music, and automatic doors. He acquired 19 supermarkets from another chain called All American, which he converted into Publix grocery stores.

In the early 1950s, Publix built its first distribution warehouse in Lakeland, Florida, which became the chain's headquarters.

By the 1960s, the stores' donut shops were converted into full bakeries and the stores began to offer delis. The chain began to expand throughout Florida. In the 1990s, it began to expand in other states.

Today, Publix has more than 750 locations throughout Florida, as well as locations in Alabama, Georgia, North Carolina, South Carolina, Tennessee, and Virginia.

What's both unique and incredible about the corporation is that it's owned by former and current employees. It's one of the largest employee-owned companies in the entire world and the largest private corporation in Florida. It also made it to *Forbes*' list of 100 Best Companies to Work for in 2017.

Pink Pineapple

You might think you'll never see a pineapple in any other color besides the golden shade we're used to, but you might be wrong. There's a pink pineapple currently in the works in the Sunshine State.

Fresh Del Monte Produce's Coral Gables division has

been working on a pink pineapple for a few years now. Called rosé pineapple, the fruit will be pink to light red inside. The patent was approved in August of 2016, but no one knows when this genetically modified fruit will end up on your grocery store shelves just yet.

As far as safety goes, the FDA has said the fruit is safe for consumption, in spite of its GMOs.

It should be interesting to see how this new—and prettier—fruit will affect America's pineapple home décor craze! Pink pineapple décor, anyone?

RANDOM FACTS

1. *USA Today* is one of the most popular newspapers today, and it started out in Cocoa Beach, Florida. The newspaper, which was originally called *Cocoa Today* back when it was released in 1966, was started by Al Neuharth. Neuharth, who previously worked for the *Miami Herald*, wanted to target NASA workers. His plan was a "breezy" newspaper for people, who, like the NASA workers, were too busy to read much. Unlike other magazines at the time, it focused more on quick to read headlines than actual stories. Over time, the newspaper became called *Florida Today* until it was finally renamed *USA Today* in 1982.

2. The *National Enquirer* and *Weekly News* both came out of Lantana, Florida. The newspapers set the stage for supermarket Hollywood tabloids and those fake celebrity news headlines. This is one invention most of us wish hadn't come out of Florida.

3. Taxol is a popular and highly effective anti-cancer drug. It was invented by Florida State University professor, Dr. Robert Holton.

4. The vaccine that's used to prevent the feline immunodeficiency virus (FIV) invented by Dr.

Janet Yamamoto from the University of Florida. Yamamoto also discovered the feline disease, which is known as "HIV for cats."

5. Bondo, which is a filler for car bodies that doesn't contain toxic lead, was invented in Miami in the 1950s. Robert Merton Spink, who owned an auto repair shop in the area, created it.

6. Acuvue contact lenses started out at Frontier Contact Lens company in Jacksonville in the 1950s. Today, the contact lenses are manufactured by Johnson & Johnson.

7. Famous Amos cookies actually started out in California, but technically Wally Amos, who founded the brand, was born and raised in Tallahassee. It was his aunt's chocolate chip cookies during his upbringing that inspired him to start the brand.

8. While he was living in Fort Myers, famous inventor Thomas Edison worked on designing commercially viable synthetic rubber to help the U.S. military gain some independence from the foreign sources they relied on for natural rubber.

9. Thomas Edison also invented the incandescent lightbulb while he was living in Fort Myers.

10. The first commercial airline started out in Florida. It flew between Tampa and St. Petersburg on a daily basis.

11. Henry Ford lived in Florida, which is where he worked on creating an affordable automobile that the average person could afford.

12. The act of streaking started out on the campus of Florida State University. Students ran across campus without their clothes on for the first time in 1973. When the press got their hands on the pictures, the fad quickly became widespread throughout the country.

13. The 1950s-style burger chain Cheeburger Cheeburger opened its first location in Sanibel Island, Florida back in 1986. The restaurant specializes in classic '50s diner foods, such as cheeseburgers, French fries, and milkshakes. Today, there more than 60 locations throughout the United States, as well as international locations in Kuwait.

14. Hard Rock Café is known for its music memorabilia and American cuisine, as well as its locations in high-tourist areas, such as casinos and cities. Hard Rock Café, Inc. is a Florida company. It was technically started in London during the 1970s, but the chain was purchased by the Seminole Tribe of Florida in 2007. Its headquarters have been in Orlando, Florida ever since.

15. Triton submarines, which produces luxury submarines, was started in Vero Beach, FL.

16. Best known for its attractive servers who dress in skimpy clothing and its famous hot wings, the Hooters restaurant chain is based in Clearwater, Florida.

17. Tibor, which produces fly fishing reels, started out in the Sunshine State. It was started in Del Ray Beach back in 1979.

18. Cardiocommand, which is best known for manufacturing blood pressure cuffs and other medical supplies, is headquartered in Tampa, FL.

19. Florida jumpstarted the modern environmental movement after John Muir was bitten by a mosquito in the state back in 1867, which led him to develop malaria. This led him to the idea that certain areas should be protected. Muir was able to convince Teddy Roosevelt to create out National Parks. It's hard to imagine what the U.S. would be like today if Muir hadn't been bitten by that mosquito!

Test Yourself – Questions and Answers

1. Who is believed to have created the first key lime recipe?

    a. Robert DeNiro
    b. Thomas Edison
    c. Sponge fishermen

2. Which restaurant chain was *not* started in Florida?

    a. Applebee's
    b. The Melting Pot
    c. Hard Rock Café

3. Which cocktail was invented in Florida?

    a. Bloody Mary
    b. Rum and coke
    c. Rum runner

4. Which popular sandwich was probably invented in Florida?

    a. Chicken parmesan sandwich
    b. Cuban sandwich
    c. Reuben sandwich

5. Which supermarket chain started out in Florida?

    a. Publix
    b. Giant
    c. Trader Joe's

Answers

1. c.
2. a.
3. c.
4. b.
5. a.

CHAPTER FIVE

FLORIDA'S BIGGEST HAUNTS, SUPERNATURAL, AND OTHER WEIRD FACTS

Florida might not seem like the most haunted location. It is nicknamed the Sunshine State, after all. But did you know that there are a number of spirits that are believed to lurk in the shadows? Do you know about any of Florida's unsolved mysteries? Have you heard about any of the creepy folklore that haunts the store? Do you know which famous serial killer was tried and executed in Florida? Do you know which Disney World attraction is said to be haunted or what other places in the Sunshine State might spook you? Have you heard about the eerie disappearances that have taken place in the state? What about the high number of homicide victims found in one region of Florida, in particular? Some of the facts you read in this chapter may be chilling. Some of them might surprise you and others are just plain weird. To find out about some of the creepiest and most bizarre things that have happened in the state of Florida, read on!

One of the Most Famous Serial Killers of All Time Was Tried and Executed in Florida

Did you know that one of the most famed serial killers of all time was both tried and electrocuted in Florida? Warning: this information may be triggering to some, as it's full of gruesome and disturbing details.

Ted Bundy murdered many young women and girls throughout the 1970s. Prior to his execution, he admitted in interviews that he killed 30 females in seven states between the years of 1974 and 1978. However, it's believed that Bundy may have actually killed even more people than what he admitted to.

Most of his victims found him to be attractive and charismatic upon meeting them in public, where he would generally fake an injury or disability or impersonate an authority figure. Once he took them to a more secluded location, he would assault and murder them. In some cases, he broke into the victims' homes and murdered them in their sleep.

After he made his kills, he would go back to the crime scenes where he would sometimes have sexual intercourse with their decomposing corpses.

At least 12 of Ted Bundy's victims were decapitated. He kept their heads as trophies in his apartment.

While he was living in Utah in 1975, Ted Bundy was incarcerated for kidnapping and assault charges.

Later, he became a prime suspect in a host of killings that had occurred across a few states. In Colorado, Ted Bundy faced murder charges, so he came up with an escape plan. He relocated to Florida where he committed three more murders before he was eventually captured. During two separate trials, Bundy was given three death sentences.

In January of 1989, he was executed in the electric chair at Florida State Prison.

A number of movies have been made about Ted Bundy.

A Florida Murder Trial Got Nationwide Attention

You've probably heard of Casey Anthony. The case took over the news headlines by storm, with *Time* magazine calling it "the social media trial of the century."

It all started out in July of 2008 when Orlando resident Cindy Anthony called 9-1-1 and reported her granddaughter, Caylee Anthony, missing for 31 days. Cindy said that a car belonging to Caylee's mother, Casey, "smelled like someone died."

Casey Anthony lied to the authorities. She said that Caylee had been kidnapped by a nanny in June but that she had been too afraid to report her daughter missing.

There was evidence suggesting that Anthony may have been responsible for the crime. Chloroform was found in the trunk of her car. There were also searches from the family's home computer on "how to make chloroform" and "neck breaking."

In October of 2008, Casey Anthony was charged with first-degree murder, to which she pled not guilty.

In December of 2008, Caylee's skeletal remains were found, along with a blanket, inside a trash bag. There was duct tape found on her face, though reports are conflicting as to where the duct tape was located.

During the six-week trial, jurors viewed 400 pieces of evidence. The prosecution sought the death penalty in the case.

The defense, which was led by Florida criminal defense attorney Jose Baez, argued that Caylee had accidentally drowned in the family pool. They claimed that Casey Anthony's father, George, covered up Caylee's death so his daughter wouldn't be charged with child neglect. Baez said this was the reason Casey hadn't done anything about her daughter being missing. The defense claimed that Casey had a habit of hiding her emotions because George Anthony had sexually abused her since she was a child.

When called to the stand, Cindy Anthony said the family had always buried their pets in plastic bags with duct tape at the closure. It was suggested that the duct tape hadn't meant to be placed on Caylee Anthony at all.

Cindy Anthony also claimed that the computer searches for chloroform and neck breaking were made by her, even though her job had on record that she was there at the time.

In July of 2011, Casey Anthony was found not guilty. The jury did, however, find her guilty of providing false information to law enforcement.

The jury's verdict was highly controversial at the time. A lot of people believed they didn't understand the meaning of "reasonable doubt," while others felt the prosecution should have built a better case. The Casey Anthony murder trial has been compared to the OJ Simpson murder trial.

To this day, Caylee Anthony's death is still considered unsolved. While most believe that Casey Anthony was responsible for the murder, others have questioned if George Anthony may have been the real culprit.

The Youngest Person to Receive Life Imprisonment is Currently Serving in Florida

The youngest person to be sentenced to life

imprisonment in America is currently incarcerated at a Florida state prison.

Lionel Tate was just 13 years old at the time of the 1999 murder. He was charged with murdering six-year-old Tiffany Eunick, who his mother was babysitting at the time. Tate was left alone with Eunick downstairs, where the two were playing.

When Tate came back upstairs, he told his mother that Eunick wasn't breathing. Tate claimed that they were wrestling and he had her in a headlock when her head hit a table.

The autopsy report, however, revealed that Tate had stomped on the girl so hard that it lacerated her liver. Eunick's skull was fractured, rib was fractured, and brain was swollen. The injuries she sustained were compared to those that one would end up with if they fell out of a three-story building.

Tate's sentence of life in prison was a controversial one. Some feel that a child of his age couldn't have known what he was doing. But under Florida Statutes, Tate was tried for first-degree murder because he knowingly abused the child, even if he hadn't intended to kill her. The prosecution didn't have to prove whether or not he knowingly committed murder.

Some also questioned if the harshness of Tate's sentence may have been due to his skin color. Was the judge harder on him because he was black?

Needless to say, the sentence was overturned in 2004. Tate's sentence was reduced to one-year house arrest and 10 years of probation.

Tate, however, broke his probation the very same year when he was found outside of his home carrying an 8" knife.

In 2005, he was charged with armed robbery when he threatened a Domino's delivery driver with a handgun at his friend's apartment. Tate also reentered the apartment, even though his friend didn't want him there. He was also charged with violating probation for having a gun.

In 2008, Tate was sentenced to 10 years in state prison. He is currently serving out his sentence at the Appalachian Correctional Institution in Sneads, Florida.

The Haunted Disney World Attraction

When you're at the Magic Kingdom, you might think it's the Haunted Mansion you need to be afraid of, but the Pirates of the Caribbean is allegedly the ride that's really haunted.

A young construction worker named George died when the ride was being built. There are conflicting stories about how he died. He either allegedly fell to his death or a heavy beam fell on his head.

Regardless of how George died, it's said that cast

members have had creepy haunted experiences with his ghost. In fact, supposedly George expects cast members to say, "Good morning," and "Goodnight," to him. What happens if they don't? Legend has it that George becomes infuriated and causes a bit of ruckus. It's believed that his ghost may shut down the ride, make calls from empty control rooms, and even show up on cameras for the ride. Workers have claimed that these odd occurrences have taken place when they've forgotten to say goodnight to George.

Park guests claim they experience a cool breeze when they're in the burning city scene of the ride, which is where George died. Cast members have claimed that the door near the scene's exit, which is now known as "George's door," repeatedly opens on its own. Some of the cast members have even claimed to feel taps on their shoulders in the section of the ride, even though no one was there.

Somehow, the Happiest Place on Earth just turned into one of the creepiest places on Earth.

Florida Has Its Very Own Bigfoot

Unless you're from the Sunshine State, there's a good chance you may have never heard of the Florida skunk ape. It's one of Florida's most popular legends.

Sometimes referred to as Florida's Bigfoot and the Swamp Cabbage Man, the skunk ape is seven-foot-tall, hairy, ape-like creature that's said to have a skunk-like odor and walk on its hind legs. Although it's said to live in several southern states, reports of sightings in Florida are said to be the most common.

Reported sightings of the skunk ape were extremely common in the 1950s and 1960s, but sightings continue to be reported in recent times. Sightings have been throughout the entire state, but particularly in Dade County and the Everglades. Florida residents, Chris Connor and Mike Barton, who run a YouTube channel, told the *Miami New Times* that they've seen the elusive creature numerous *times* in Green Swamp, which lies between Orlando and Tampa.

There's a well-known skunk ape hunter in Florida. Dave Shealy runs Skunk Ape Headquarters, which is located in the Florida Everglades. His business consists of an airboat, adventure tour, and gift shop, all centered on the urban legend. Due to his interesting line of work, he has been featured on the Discovery Channel and *Unsolved Mysteries*.

Shealy's family has allegedly between in the area since the 1800s. He claims that the Florida skunk ape has been spotted for centuries. According to Shealy, a Miccosukee tribal elder once told him that the Native Americans tried to communicate with the skunk apes, in hopes that they could help them win the fight over their land. Their attempts at communication were unsuccessful, however.

So, what exactly *is* the Florida skunk ape? That's the question everyone wants to know the answer to. Some believe the Florida Skunk Ape might just be a not so distant cousin of Bigfoot. One woman anonymously sent pictures of the skunk ape to the Sarasota County Sheriff's Department. The woman, who claimed the skunk ape had come to her yard and stolen her apples from a tree, believed the creature to be an escaped orangutan.

Of course, there are skeptics. Paranormal investigator Joe Nickell is highly skeptical of the folklore and believes that the reported sightings of the creature are most likely black bears. The United States Park Service, of course, claims the Skunk Ape is just a hoax.

Regardless of what it is, let's hope to never come face-to-face with one (or maybe you want to, who knows).

The Legend of Robert the Doll

Have you ever heard of the haunted doll? No, we're not talking about Chucky. This doll is named Robert and the story might creep you out a little.

The doll was originally owned by an artist by the name of Robert Eugene Otto. Otto belonged to a wealthy family in Key West.

There are a couple of stories about how young Otto came to own the doll. Some say that Otto's grandfather brought the doll back from Germany in 1904. Others say that the doll came from Otto's nanny, who practiced voodoo. Other stories say that a young girl from the Bahamas gave Otto the doll.

Regardless of how Robert acquired it, he owned a doll, which stood 41" inch tall and wore a sailor suit. Robert named the doll after itself.

According to local legend, the doll was haunted. It allegedly moved, smiled, giggled, and even talked to Robert.

Some believe the doll had supernatural abilities. Others believe the doll was cursed. Some even believe that Otto somehow awakened the doll's magical powers.

Although the doll was said to have been Otto's best friend, the doll apparently wasn't always nice. People said the doll caused crashes to crash, bones to break, people to lose their jobs, couples to get divorced, and other misfortunes.

Today, the doll can be found on display at the Martello Gallery-Key West Art and Historical Museum. Legend says that museum visitors are at risk of experiencing misfortunes of their own if they don't "respect" Robert, so be nice to the doll if you have the opportunity to visit his exhibit. According to local lore, you're supposed to ask Robert's permission before you take his picture.

Robert the Doll has made a few appearances besides

the museum. It appeared on the Travel Channel show *Zak Bagans: Mystery Mansion*. It was also featured in an episode of the TV show *Lore*.

A horror movie about the doll, called *Robert*, was also released in 2015. There have also been a few sequels to the movie: 2016's *The Curse of Robert the Doll*, 2017's *The Toymaker*, and *The Revenge of Robert the Doll*, which is set for release in 2018.

The St. Augustine Lighthouse is Said to Be Haunted

St. Augustine is often said to be every ghost hunter's dream. The town is full of plenty of allegedly haunted places, including the Spanish Military Hospital and the Old Jail. But one of the most popular haunted places in the St. Augustine Lighthouse, which *Coastal Living* ranks as one of the "Top to Haunted Lighthouses" in the U.S.

Built in 1874, this charming lighthouse is a favorite among those seeking ghostly encounters. People have reported paranormal activity at St. Augustine Lighthouse, ranging from eerie sounds, unexplained cool sensations, and even seeing apparitions. People have also claimed to hear footsteps on the tower stairs, even though there's no one there.

The St. Augustine Lighthouse is said to be home to a number of ghosts. For starters, there's the ghost of Peter Rasmussen, who one of the first lighthouse keepers. Rasmussen allegedly loved cigars. Both staff and guests have reported smelling cigars. The reports of the cigar smells began shortly after his death.

Another deceased lighthouse keeper, Joseph Andreu, had a fatal fall while he was painting the lighthouse tower. People have claimed to see Andreu's ghost at the top of the lighthouse.

Then there are the ghosts of Eliza and Mary Pity, who drowned in the late 1800s while their mom was renovating the lighthouse. People claim to hear laughter from the sisters late at night. Some have even claimed to see an apparition who wears the same blue velvet dress one of the girls was wearing on the day of her death.

The St. Augustine Lighthouse & Museum website even acknowledges the fact that seven people have died on their grounds. If this doesn't prove the place could be haunted, I'm not sure what does!

Tallahassee May Have Had Its Own Witch Hunt

When you think of witch hunts, you likely think of Salem, Massachusetts—not Tallahassee, Florida. However, there's a good possibility that a woman who was killed for suspicions of being a witch may be buried in Tallahassee's Old City Cemetery.

Although no historical records officially confirm it for sure, there are a number of signs that the townspeople thought 23-year-old Elizabeth "Bessie" Budd-Graham was a witch. For starters, her grave faces west, which goes against Christian tradition—as well as the other gravestones in the cemetery, which all face east.

Many consider the strangest part to be the fact that Edgar Allen Poe's "Lenore" is the epitaph on her tombstone, which references both vampires and witches (and how they need to be killed twice).

And then there are the legends, which say that Elizabeth put a spell on her husband so he would marry her and that she was a good witch who only practiced love and protection spells.

No one will ever really know for sure if she was a witch, but to this day, Wiccans visit Bessie's grave to leave gifts for her.

Lots of UFO Sightings Are Reported in Florida

Unsurprisingly, Florida ranks No. 2 on the list of states with the highest number of UFO sightings. With NASA's Kennedy Space Center in the state, it makes you wonder how many of the sightings are government-related and how many of them are extraterrestrial.

According to the National UFO Reporting Center, there have been more than 6,000 reports of UFO sightings in Florida since 1998—and about 1,000 of those have taken place since 2015. The only state with a higher number of sightings is California.

Perhaps the most well-known alleged sighting out of Florida took place in November of 1987. Known as the Gulf Breeze Sightings, a contractor named Ed Walters submitted photos of what was allegedly a UFO to the *Gulf Breeze Sentinel*. The photos gained nationwide attention and were even featured on *Unsolved Mysteries*. However, many believe the photos to have been a hoax.

Regardless of its legitimacy, plenty of Floridians continue to report UFOs they've spotted. In 2017, someone reported a sighting of a rectangular unidentified flying object over Tampa Bay that made headlines. In 2018, there have been alleged sightings in Orlando. South Florida is said to be a hot spot for UFO sightings.

Florida Was Rumored to Have a Fountain of Youth

Maybe you've read or seen *Tuck Everlasting*, but have you ever considered the possibility that a Fountain of Youth might really be out there? Rumor has it that the Fountain of Youth might be located in Florida. At least, that's what Spanish explorer Juan Ponce de León really believed when he discovered the region.

When he traveled to Florida in 1513, the explorer was allegedly searching for the Fountain of Youth. When he got there, Native Americans supposedly told him the Fountain of Youth was located in Bimini. No one's ever discovered the fountain, though—or if they have, they've kept it to themselves.

The Legend of the Devil's Chair

Have you ever heard of a town called Cassadaga, Florida? Some might call it one of the creepiest towns in the country, let alone in Florida.

Cassadaga, which is located north of Deltona, has been named the "Psychic Capital of the World." This is because a lot of psychics and mediums live—and work—in the town. Many of them work out of the Cassadaga Hotel, which is well-known for its psychic readings. The hotel is also said to be haunted, with the first floor allegedly being home to many spirits.

The town is also known for something even eerier: The Devil's Chair.

The "chair" is actually a brick bench, which is located in a cemetery, that legend says was built by the devil himself. The devil allegedly comes to sit on his chair every night at midnight. You might be tempted to sit on the Devil's Chair, but you probably shouldn't. Legend says that you'll forever be haunted by the devil if you sit on his chair. It's even been said that if you leave a full can of opened beer and return to the bench the following morning, the beer will be gone—

even though the can will be left unopened.

Henry Flagler is Said to Haunt Flagler College

Henry Flagler played a key role in the history of Florida's development. Known as the "Father of Miami and Palm Beach," Flagler founded the Florida East Coast Railway. Did you know his spirit is still said to reside in the state?

Flagler College was built around what was originally Ponce de Leon Hotel, which was a hotel that Henry Flagler opened in St. Augustine. Flagler is said to have loved the hotel he built.

The legend goes like this: Flagler died in Palm Beach in 1913, his body was laid in the hotel's rotunda. Rumor has it that when it time for his body to be carried out, all of the doors in the hotel slammed.

Henry Flagler's body was buried at the local mausoleum, but a lot of people believe that his spirit stayed at the Ponce de Leon.

Another legend says that Flagler was trapped in the rotunda and that his spirit lingered to keep an eye on the property he was so proud of.

It's believed that Henry Flagler's spirit isn't the only one that haunted the hotel. People also believe that Ponce de Leon Hall at Flagler College is also home to the spirits of both Flagler's second wife, Ida Alicia, and his mistress, whose spirit is said to take the form of "a woman in black."

It's been said that the spirits of these women aren't always the friendliest. The woman in black, who was allegedly a frequent hotel visitor who Henry Flagler allegedly had an affair with, is believed to be an angry ghost. Flagler wanted to keep her hidden from his wife and allegedly locked her in a room on the 4th floor, which supposedly led the woman to go crazy and hang herself. Today, the 4th floor is used for student housing. Students have reported hearing screams, things being thrown off the walls, and other ghostly activity in the room.

Ida Alicia, on the other hand, allegedly knew about her husband's affair. It's said that this drove her mad. Ida suffered from bipolar disorder and spent time in a sanitorium before eventually dying from tuberculosis. Nowadays, students report seeing what they believe to be her ghost staring at the paintings in the hall of the college, including one where Henry Flagler once stood.

Florida's I-4 "Dead Zone"

Have you ever heard of Florida's "Dead Zone"? Well, after reading this, you might wish that you hadn't. This is pretty creepy.

There's an overpass on 1nterstate-4, which is known as the "Dead Zone." Located just north of Orlando at the St. John's River in Seminole County, this area of the highway earned this name for two reasons. We'll get to the second reason in a bit, but the first reason it's called that is that it rests above four graves.

It all dates back to 1887 when an epidemic of yellow fever broke out in the area, killing four family members who lived in a small Roman Catholic colony. The colony's priest had died from yellow fever, which left no one to administer the family their last rites. Instead, they were buried without any sort of ceremony.

In 1905, Albert Hawkins purchased the land and found the graves when he had the property cleared for farming. He farmed around the graves, leaving them in the center of the field like an island on the farm. His farm was known as the "Field of the Dead," though it remained a secret within the community.

After Albert Hawkins died in 1939, his widow remained the owner of the property. In 1960, the land was purchased by the state of Florida, who had plans to build Interstate-4. While State surveyors were made aware of the graves, they weren't removed from the area. Instead, the graves were covered with dirt to provide elevation for I-4.

Here's where things start to get really creepy. When the state covered the graves with dirt, Hurricane Donna crossed the state. Florida is prone to hurricanes so that in itself might not be so strange, but here's what *is* strange: the hurricane, which had appeared to be heading westward to the Gulf of Mexico completely changed paths, and the eye of the storm passed right over the family's graves. The hurricane caused a lot of flooding to the area, which disrupted to construction on the highway for months. A lot of people in the area thought Hurricane Donna's strange path had to do with highway construction workers building over the graves.

Unfortunately, the strangeness doesn't end there. People have reported their cell phones picking up on strange voices when they reach the south end of the I-4 bridge in Seminole County. One woman even reported that her phone calls have been interrupted by "voices of the dead." There have also been reports of static on car radios and sightings of "white mist" and "balls of light" on this area of the interstate. People have even claimed to see ghost hitchhikers (hitchhikers but in apparition form) in the area. All very creepy, but things get even scarier than that.

The second reason this area of I-4 is known as the "Dead Zone"? This stretch of the highway is known for an unusually high number of accidents.

The Haunted Cuban Club

Have you ever heard of the Cuban Club? If you're a ghost hunter, you just might want to check it out. The

Cuban Club is said to only be one of the most haunted places in all of Florida but one of the most haunted places in all of the world! The *Travel Channel* has listed it as one of the 10 most haunted places.

The Cuban Club, which is located in Ybor City, was built in 1917 after a lot of Cuban immigrants made their way into the area. Before it was built, there was another clubhouse in the area, but it burnt down in a fire.

The Cuban Club, which was restored, features a ballroom, cantina, gymnasium, pharmacy, bowling alley, swimming pool, library, and two-story theater. You might not think it looks like such a creepy place, but the Cuban Club is said to be haunted. In fact, it has even earned the nickname "Club Dead."

It has been confirmed that at least two people have died at the Cuban Club. One of those deaths took place in the 1920s when an actor, whose name is said to have been Vincent, committed suicide at the theater. Rumor has it that he even did it onstage in front of an audience.

The second death occurred when one of the club's board members murdered another board member. The board member's body was found in the boardroom after an argument led one of the board members to deliver a fatal shot to the other board member's face.

It's said that the spirits of both the actor and the board

member haunt the Cuban Club, but reports are more frequently made about Vincent. People have reported seeing the spirit of the actor in the bathroom mirror. The spirit is said to speak both English and Spanish. Vincent the actor allegedly spoke fluently in both languages. People have reported that he's talked to them about how hard he's worked for his career as an actor, only to end up working at the Cuban Club, and asks people to give him a reason not to commit suicide. Creepy, to say the least.

People have also reported seeing other spirits at the Cuban Club. There have been numerous reports of a woman in white wearing red heels. She's said to climb up and down the stairs and is often heard wailing. There's also a piano that allegedly plays without any sitting at it. People have reported seeing orbs of light.

One of the other most well-known ghosts at the Cuban Club is that of a boy. It's believed that he may be the ghost of an 8-year-old boy who drowned at a pool in the Cantina. People claim to see him and hear him making an array of noises, such as playing with balls and opening and closing doors.

Perhaps the creepiest thing of all? People have reported smelling wood-burning when they experience paranormal activity at the Cuban Club. Could they be smelling this wood burning due to the club's history of being built overtop a building that had previously burned down?

The Florida Theater May Be Haunted

Another one of the most haunted places in Florida is said to be the Florida Theatre in Jacksonville. The theater, which was built in 1926, is said to be home to its very own spirit!

The spirit is believed to be that of Doc Crowther, who was one of the theater's early motion picture technicians. Employees have reportedly seen strange shadows in the theater balcony or caught unexplained lights in photos.

The lights at the theater are said to go out when the spirit is upset. One of the theater's workers told the *Jax Daily Record* that she once warned a group of children not to go near the theater's projector due to the spirit and mentioned the issue with the lights. The children didn't believe her and, as if to prove it, the lights went out at the moment. When the children moved away from the projector, the light went back on.

The Florida Theatre is so well-known for being haunted that Channel 7 even had a psychic called in to try to make a connection with the spirit—and she did. According to psychic, Jill Cook-Richards, the spirit even spoke with her. The spirit allegedly claimed that he wanted to be called "J," short for joy—an emotion that he has for the theater.

It gets even creepier. Theater workers had another psychic brought in and she, too, said the spirit called itself "J."

RANDOM FACTS

1. This may seem a bit silly, but it's one of Florida's most talked about urban legends. Back in the 1950s and 1960s, people near the Tomoka River, which is near Daytona Beach, claimed they were chased out of the woods. It was a strange pink cloud that supposedly drove them out. As the tale goes, the allegedly carnivorous cloud would swallow people and then spit out their bones. Watch out for any pink clouds the next time you're in the Daytona Beach area.

2. The Key West Cemetery is known to be haunted. The cemetery's location was founded in 1847, but there was another cemetery on the grounds previously. A hurricane wiped out most of the old cemetery, causing the dead to be scattered throughout the forest. The gravestones from the old cemetery were moved after the hurricane to the highest point in the cemetery. These gravestones are, therefore, older than the Key West Cemetery itself, dating back to 1829 and 1843. It has been said that a lot of paranormal activity occurs at the cemetery. The spirit of a woman from the Bahamas, who is said to haunt the cemetery, acts as the guardian. The spirit is said to approach

visitors who she feels are being disrespectful to the dead, so be nice! Strange voices, unexplained voices, and weird orbs of light are often reported.

3. The Daytona Beach serial killer, who murdered at least four women in the Daytona Beach area between 2005 and 2007, is still on the loose. Three of his victims were believed to be prostitutes, while another wasn't (though she did have a drug problem). No possible suspects have been named, though police have randomly swabbed motorists fitting the profile of a white male believed to be behind the murders.

4. Fort Lauderdale is said to be haunted. It even made the Travel Channel's list of most haunted cities in America. The New River Inn, which is the Old Fort Lauderdale History Museum, is said to be the city's creepiest spot. Locals say a ghost guards the museum at night. The ghost is said to be that of P. N. Bryan's, who once owned the museum. Some other supposedly haunted places in Fort Lauderdale include Lucky's Tavern, King-Cromartie House, the River House, and the Strahan House.

5. The historic Renaissance Vinoy Hotel in St. Petersburg is said to be haunted. Major League Baseball players, who sometimes stay at the hotel when playing in Tampa, have experienced some odd and potentially paranormal occurrences.

Flickering lights, doors slamming, and the apparition of a man wearing a tuxedo and top hat have all been reported.

6. There's a myth that the government tried to stop the mosquito problem in Florida by releasing what we know of as "lovebugs" today. Apparently, the goal was to create a female bug that would distract male mosquitoes to prevent them from breeding. Things allegedly went awry when a male lovebug was accidentally created, which just added to Florida's bug problem. The question is: is it *really* a myth?

7. Many people are unaware that there are hundreds of wild Rhesus monkeys, which live in Silver Springs State Park.

8. There's a gravity hill in Lake Wales where cars roll uphill while in neutral. Although scientists have found ways to explain gravity hills, they always come with some crazy legends. As the tale goes, there was a battle between a giant alligator and a Native American chief, which ended in death for both of them. This caused a sinkhole to form in the area. After the road was paved, people began to experience the gravity hill. The hill is referred to as "Spook Hill" by locals.

9. If you're ever in Lady Lakes, Florida, you might want to stay away from Rolling Acres Road. If

you turn west on the road, your car might begin to malfunction—even if you have a new vehicle. Local lore says that the hood of the car will fill with white smoke and the car will stop working for at least 10 minutes, leaving you stranded in the woods. People who get stranded claim to hear screams and groans coming from the woods. The road is said to be haunted by the ghost of Julia, who was allegedly murdered by a jealous boyfriend. Legend says that she roams the woods until she's approached, in which case her eyes will glow red and she'll scream bloody murder. If you do happen to end up stranded on Rolling Acres Road, it's best to stay in your vehicle until it starts again.

10. The Fairchild Oak, which is sometimes called "Haunted Oak" by locals, is located at Bulow Creek State Park in Ormond Beach, is no doubt a beautiful sight to see. However, it's also believed to be one of the scariest, especially for people who are alone. Urban legend says that the tree whispers to lone travelers, which cause them to take their own lives. To make matters even creepier, two people have died at Fairchild Oak. Norman Harwood committed suicide. James Ormond II's dead body was found at the tree and, while his death remains a mystery, it's believed that he, too, killed himself.

11. The Oviedo Lights are one of Oviedo's local legends. The lights, which are said to be spotted on Snow Hill Road on the bridge leading to the Econlockhatchee River, are often called the "Oviedo Ghost Lights." While they might appear as headlights, the lights are said to be as bright as a freight train. Although reports of the lights were most frequent during the 1940s and 1970s, they're still reported in recent times. What are the lights exactly? A few local legends have been used as possible theories. Some people believe they're caused by the ghost of a young guy who was supposedly decapitated while he was with his lover. Others think they might be the spirit of a supposed Cub scout who disappeared. Some believe the lights are caused by swamp gas. Scientists from the physics department at the University of Florida tried to figure out the cause, but they didn't come up with any possible explanation. Whatever the cause is, travelers should drive the road with caution or find a different route. It's been said that the lights have caused many drivers to get into accidents, some of which have been fatal. What's even spookier is that there have been reports of noises that sound like a woman being strangled at night.

12. The Bloody Bucket Bridge is considered one of Florida's creepiest urban legends. When driving

down Reinhart Pass Road in Wauchula, you will come to the bridge. It got its name as the "Bloody Bucket Bridge" because local legend says that the water turns red, like blood, at certain times when there's moonlight. What time is it seen? No one can remember, apparently. So, what causes the blood to turn red? And how did the bridge get its name? If you ask the town locals, the story is a little far-fetched, but it goes like this: the blood is from the babies who were killed by a midwife in the area. The midwife allegedly smothered babies when she was afraid that their families couldn't afford them and buried their bodies in the woods near the river. As the tale goes, the spirits of the babies whose lives she took came to haunt her. They would fill a bucket in her home with their blood to remind her of what she had done. She would go down to the river every day to empty it, but it would be full again by the time she got back home. This happened until she slipped and drowned in the river one day when she went to empty the bucket. Since her death, the river continued to turn a bloody shade of red to remind people in Wauchula of the babies they lost.

13. Maybe Florida really *is* home to the devil. Not only is the state hot, but this is the 2nd landmark in the state that has his name. The Devil's Tree, which is located in at Oak Hammock Park in Port

St. Lucie, appears like an ordinary oak tree but it's anything but. Two teenage girls were killed and buried there back in the 1970s. Thanks to its name, a lot of Satan worshippers have smeared the tree with blood they use in sacrifices. With such a dark history, it's no surprise that evil is said to lurk there. People have reported hearing strange sounds in the area and some have even claimed to see ghosts at the tree. Most people also claim to feel a cooling, spine-chilling sensation when they stand in front of the tree.

14. The Arcadia Opera House is said to be another one of Florida's most haunted places. The *Bravo* TV network even set its paranormal team out to investigate the opera house. The opera house has a long history. It was built in 1905 after a fire destroyed most of the downtown area in Arcadia. While the opera house is most recognized as being a museum and antique shop today, it has had many different uses over the years, including a USO operation during World War II. There have been reports of ghostly laughter and footsteps. A child once reportedly entered the room, but no child was ever seen—though a spirit was felt. People have claimed to see a number of ghosts, including the apparition of a crying young girl, a ghost in the auditorium hallway, and the ghost of a girl in a 2nd-floor window. There

haven't been any deaths at the opera house that would explain any of these paranormal occurrences, which makes the ghostly activity even stranger. No one knows for sure what's causing these supposed ghosts to haunt the Arcadia Opera House.

15. Located in Jackson's County, Sunland was a hospital used for treating TB and then later mentally disabled children. The now-defunct hospital, which was built in 1952, was known to mistreat its patients. After many reports of abuse and neglect, Sunland closed in 1983. The facility's previous employees allegedly have such bad memories of the abuse endured at the hospital that they refuse to even set foot on the hospital grounds. In 1997, the elevator was destroyed after a guy fell down the elevator shaft. A lot of strange photos of the abandoned property are floating around the internet, however, which depict strange blurs that may belong to spirits. People who have visited the former hospital site are also generally convinced of a paranormal presence. People reportedly hear children's laughter and see unexplained light orbs. It's also been said that the swings at the park on the property move on their own. It seems safe to say that the spirits seem to be at unrest, since screams and shrieking have been heard on the property at night.

16. The May-Stringer House, which is currently the Hernando Heritage Museum, is another one of the Sunshine State's most haunted places. The May-Stringer House is a historic location in Brooksville, Florida, which is said to be home to ghosts. The land was purchased back in the 1850s by a contractor named John L. May. He lived in the house, which he built for his family, until his death from tuberculosis. His wife Marena continued to live in the house throughout the Civil War. She later remarried Frank Saxon, a Confederate war hero. Marena tragically died during childbirth. The child, Jessie Mae, survived, but died at three years old. John May, Marena, Jessie, and an infant son of Frank and Marena were all buried on the property. Frank Saxon eventually sold the house to Dr. Sheldon Stringer. The house was used as both the home and the practice of the doctor. The Stringer family continued to live in the house until they all had died. After they were gone, the house had several owners until the Hernando Historical Museum Association bought the property in 1980 and did restorations on the mansion. Since then, there have been numerous reports of paranormal activity from the May-Stringer House and grounds. People have claimed to feel unusually cool air, see unexplained orbs of light, hear a child (believed to be Jessie Mae) crying, and see mists, strange shadows, and ghostly apparitions.

17. The Biltmore Hotel in Coral Gables is believed to be one of the most haunted hotels in all of Florida. Gangster Thomas "Fatty" Walsh was shot at the hotel in 1929 as the result of a gambling dispute. Fatty's ghost is believed to haunt the hotel, with the bar being his most frequent haunting spot. There have been reports of the glasses and bottles on the bar shelves shaking without any possible explanation. The ghost of Fatty has been spotted on the 13th floor of the Biltmore—the same floor he was killed on—and in hotel mirrors. Women have also picked up on the scent of cigar smoke—which is believed to be because they're being followed around by Fatty, who was known to love his both Cuban cigars and women. It's believed that Fatty is a good spirit. His spirit isn't the only one that's believed to haunt the Biltmore Hotel, though. In the 1930s—ten years after Fatty's murder—a woman allegedly went missing after she was last seen walking outside the Biltmore Hotel. It's believed that her spirit may be responsible for the unexplained swinging doors and strange noises that have been seen and heard by the hotel's kitchen staff. The Biltmore has an annual Halloween party you might want to check out if you want to experience some paranormal activity.

18. The Deering Estate, which encompasses 444 acres, is said to be an active spot for paranormal activity.

There's a Historic Ghost Stories tour, which takes guests through the paths that were taken by the Native Americans and estate owner Charles Deering. A psychic who took the tour claimed to hear a woman begging for help to save a child who was drowning. In 1925, Deering died on the land, which is believed to be haunted by his spirit. People have claimed to see his apparition. The Deering Estate hosts a Spookover, which is an overnight haunted tour during the month of October. Guests are taken on a tour of the areas of the estate which are known to experience the most paranormal activity. When you visit Deering Estate, you're encouraged to bring your own equipment to detect paranormal activity. See if any ghosts show up in your cameras, if you can hear them on your voice recorders, etc.

19. Did you know that Florida is said to have its own Bermuda Triangle? The theory came about because a number of planes have mysteriously disappeared near the Florida Everglades. In 1945, five training patrol Grumman Avenger aircrafts disappeared. The incident is one of the most well-known airplane disappearances of all time. No one ever discovered what might have happened to the aircrafts, and no wreckage has ever been found. The squadron was given the name "The Lost Patrol." And to add even more credibility to

the theory of a Bermuda Triangle in the Everglades? A Navy plane was sent to the area in an attempt to rescue them. The only problem? The Navy plane went missing, too...

20. While the Everglades is one of the most beautiful regions in the country with its natural beauty and unique wildlife, there's also something really creepy about it. The Everglades is a popular body dumping grounds. Both law enforcement and people walking through the area have stumbled upon bodies, some of which were killed in some of the most gruesome ways possible. From gun wounds and body mutilations to people who were burned to death, the Everglades have been used to cover up all sorts of murders. Some bodies have also been found floating in the rivers of the Everglades. To put it into perspective, there have been more than 175 victims of homicide found in the Everglades. And those were the bodies that were found. It's believed that there are probably more bodies out there, just waiting to be found...

Test Yourself – Questions and Answers

1. Which of the Devil's spots is *not* said to be located in Florida?

    a. The Devil's Seat
    b. The Devil's Chair
    c. The Devil's Tree

2. In terms of states with the highest number of UFO sightings, Florida ranks:

    a. No. 1
    b. No. 2
    c. No. 49

3. The Biltmore Hotel is thought to be haunted by which gangster?

    a. Pretty Boy Floyd
    b. Al Capone
    c. Thomas "Fatty" Walsh

4. Florida's Bermuda Triangle is thought to be located near ____.

    a. Jacksonville
    b. Daytona Beach
    c. The Everglades

5. Which city may have convicted, killed, and buried a young woman for being a witch?

    a. Miami
    b. Tallahassee
    c. Jacksonville

Answers

1. a.
2. b.
3. c.
4. c.
5. b.

CHAPTER SIX

FLORIDA'S SPORTS

Did you know that Florida is often called the "Sports Capital of the World"? The sports industry has a huge economic impact on the state, bringing in more than $57 billion, attracting more than 15 million visitors from out of state every year, and providing 580,000 jobs. But what else do you know about sports in Florida? Did you know that the NASCAR 500 takes place in Daytona, but did you know the drivers don't do 500 laps? Do you know how many laps they really do? You know the Sunshine State is home to the Miami Dolphins, but do you know which NFL legend was once a part of the team? Hint: there was more than one! Do you know which famous athlete sisters did their training in the state or which of the world's largest races takes place in the state? Do you know which golf legend calls the state his home? To find out the answer to these and other questions, read on.

NASCAR Started Out in Florida

Did you know that NASCAR got its start in the Sunshine State?

It all started out back in 1930 when a mechanic named Bill France stopped in Daytona Beach—and decided to never leave. France opened an auto repair shop, where he spent his spare time working on cars with one goal in mind: making them faster.

By the mid-1930s, people were having record-speed races on Daytona Beach. Bill, who was one of those racers, decided to start charging spectators for the events. After he made some money from the events, he began to promote races in North and South Carolina.

In 1947, Bill France created the foundation for a national series of races. The name? The National Association for Stock Car Automobile Racing—otherwise known as NASCAR.

Racing in Daytona is much different today than it was prior to the creation of NASCAR. The Daytona Beach Road Course, where France held the original races, is no longer used by the foundation. NASCAR races now take place at Daytona International Speedway, which opened in 1959.

The Daytona International Speedway tri-oval track encompasses 180 acres, with the infield being large enough to hold two Disneyland theme parks *and* a lake of its own. It's a sight to be seen, especially for those who love NASCAR!

The Daytona 500 Isn't Really 500 Laps

Did you know that racers don't do 500 laps at the Daytona 500? While true NASCAR fans know this, most of the general population does not.

The race actually consists of 200 laps, though there's a chance it could be cut short due to weather conditions and it has gone over a few extra laps to get a fair winner.

You're probably wondering what the "500" in the Daytona 500 means if it doesn't mean the driver has to do 500 laps. The 500 is referring to the actual distance of the race, which is 500 miles. During the 200 laps, the drivers will drive 2.5-mile circuits. By the end of the race, the driver will have driven 500 miles (sometimes a little less or a little more).

It takes approximately three hours for NASCAR drivers to finish the race.

Daytona 500 Victories

The Daytona 500 is what some consider to be the most significant NASCAR event that's held each year. Whether you're a NASCAR fan or not, you might be wondering about some of the event's biggest victors.

The first Daytona 500 was won by Lee Petty. It wasn't

easy for race officials to determine this either, as Petty finished nearly neck-in-neck with other competitors. It actually took officials *three days* to determine who the winner was based on what was depicted in a photo of the finish line.

Lee Petty's son, Richard, won the most Daytona 500 races in NASCAR history. He won the trophy seven times throughout his NASCAR career. Richard and Lee Petty both competed in the first Daytona 500 Richard ever competed in, but neither of them won the event.

Bill Elliott takes the record for the fastest driver in the history of the Daytona 500. In 1987, Ford driver Elliott completed one lap in a matter of 42.78 seconds, with an average speed of 210.36 mph. In 1988, NASCAR came up with a rule for the Daytona 500 that stated engine horsepower needed to be reduced in order to keep speeds down. It seems likely that Bill Elliott just may hold his record until the end of time.

NASCAR Legend Dale Earnhardt Died During the Daytona 500

Did you know that NASCAR racing legend Dale Earnhardt died during the Daytona 500 in February of 2001?

Dale Earnhardt was born into a racing family. His father, Ralph Earnhardt, won a NASCAR Sportsman

Championship in 1956.

Dale Earnhardt has been named as one of the 50 best NASCAR drivers of all time, which comes as no surprise. Earnhardt set a number of records throughout the course of his racing career. Some of his career highlights include:

- A total of 76 Winston Cup race wins.
- Winner of the 1998 Daytona 500.
- Winner of seven NASCAR Winston Cup championships, tying with only Richard Petty for this record, which he made in 1998. (As of 2016, Jimmie Johnson also ties with them).

Tragically, Dale Earnhardt was killed in 2001 after colliding with Sterling Marlin during the Daytona 500. The collision happened during the final lap of the race. Sterling Martin survived.

Earnhardt was inducted into the NASCAR Hall of Fame in 2010.

NFL Legend Dan Marino Played for the Miami Dolphins

Former Miami Dolphins player Dan Marino is regarded as one of the best NFL quarterbacks of all time, but his path to success wasn't always an easy one.

Marino played college football at the University of Pittsburgh. His reputation took a hit due to alleged rumors of drug use, but the Miami Dolphins still chose him during the draft in 1983—but there were five other quarterbacks chosen ahead of him. Even so, Marino proved himself to be the best.

During his rookie year with the Dolphins, Marino led the team to a 12-4 record. The NFL star also scored 20 touchdowns and became the first rookie to be a starting quarterback at the Pro Bowl, at which he was named NFL's Rookie of the Year.

The next season, Marino had his best year—and one of the best ever seasons by any quarterback in the history of the NFL. Scoring 48 touchdowns, Marino also threw for more than 5,000 yards and led the team to the Super Bowl (though the team did lose to the 49ers).

Dan Marino retired from the NFL in 2000, making for a total of 17 years in the league.

In 2005, Marino was inducted into the Pro Bowl Hall of Fame.

And it's all thanks to Miami Dolphins taking a chance on him, even despite analysts saying it wasn't the best decision at the time!

10 Miami Dolphins Players Have Been Inducted into the Hall of Fame

Did you know that 10 Miami Dolphins Players have been inducted into the Pro Football Hall of Fame?

The team's Hall of Famers include:

1. Paul Warfield
2. Larry Csonka
3. Jim Langer
4. Bob Griese
5. Larry Little
6. Don Shula
7. Dwight Stephenson
8. Nick Buoniconti
9. Dan Marino
10. Thurman Thomas

NFL Player Tim Tebow Got His Start in Florida

Today he's a household name, but did you know that Tim Tebow got his start in Florida? In fact, some have considered Tebow to be one of the best—if not *the* best—athlete to have ever gotten his start in the Sunshine State.

Tim Tebow grew up in Jacksonville, Florida. Though he was homeschooled, Tim was able to play football for the local high school, the Trinity Christian Academy. He played tight end.

He later played quarterback for Allen D. Nease High School, whose football team was struggling. Tebow's running and throwing abilities helped gain him national attention. While he suffered from a knee injury that kept him out of the game his junior season,

Tebow was still named Florida's Player of the Year. This title made him sought after by college football team.

During his senior high school season, Tebow led the Nease Panthers to state title. Tebow also earned All-State honors. He was again named Florida's Player of the Year, made it into *Parade* magazine, earned the title of Florida's Mr. Football, and played in the U.S. Army All-American Bowl as one of the top 78 high school football players in the country. An ESPN *Faces in Sports* documentary even focused on him in a segment called *Tim Tebow: The Chosen One*.

Tim Tebow went on to play for the Florida Gators at the University of Florida, the school both of his parents had attended. Tebow's freshman year was spent as a backup for the Gators, but he saw much success with the team as starting quarterback. Tebow became the first sophomore to ever win Heisman Trophy in 2007. He led the Gators to a BCS championship in 2008. Tim Tebow is also the only Florida Gator to ever be named MVP three times.

From 2010 to 2012, Tebow played for the Denver Broncos. In 2012, he also played for the New York Jets.

And to think it all started with that 1996 legislation in Florida that let homeschooled kids compete in high school sporting events!

The Williams Sisters Trained in Florida

Venus and Serena Williams are legendary women's tennis stars. Did you know the famous tennis sisters trained in Florida?

The Williams family was originally living in Compton, California when the sisters' talent was discovered. To ensure the girls both got the best tennis training possible, their parents moved them to West Palm Beach, Florida when Serena was nine and Venus was 10.

In Florida, the girls trained at Rick Macci's academy. He also coached the sisters privately because he recognized their talent. However, William's father eventually pulled the girls out of the academy after hearing parents from the academy talking badly about their race. He also wanted his daughters to focus on their schoolwork. He continued to train the sisters at home.

By the time both sisters were 14, they had both made their professional tennis debuts and today are considered some of the best women's tennis stars of all time!

NFL Legend Emmitt Smith Started Out in Florida

Did you know that Emmitt Smith is from Florida?

Emmitt Smith, who is recognized at the NFL's all-time leading rusher, is from Pensacola. Smith attended

Escambia High School in Pensacola. He played high school football and also ran track.

While Emmitt Smith was in high school, the team won the state championship. Smith set a record: he rushed for 106 touchdowns and total of 8,804 yards, the 2nd most yardage of any high school football player at the time.

In 1986, the *USA Today* and *Parade* magazine named Emmitt Smith the high school player of the year.

Even though Smith accomplished a lot during his high school football career, college recruiters believed he was too small and too slow to experience college football success.

Nevertheless, Smith received an athletic scholarship to the University of Florida, where he played for the Florida Gators. He played for the team for three seasons.

While playing for the Gators, Smith broke the team's single-game rushing record when he carried 39 times for 224 yards and made two touchdowns. During his freshman year in 1987, he finished with 1,341 yards, was named the National Freshman of the Year and finished 9th in Heisman voting.

When Smith suffered from a knee injury, along with another player, the team struggled. When Smith returned, the Gators still managed to finish the season

7-5. They won in the 1988 All-American Bowl, where Smith ran a 55-yard touchdown and earned the title of MVP in the game.

Emmitt Smith later went on to get drafted for the Dallas Cowboys, who he spent 13 out of 15 years of his NFL career with. Smith holds the NFL title for rushing yards; he has a total of 18,355 rushing yards. It's thought to be unlikely that anyone will ever break him of this record.

In 2010, Emmitt Smith was inducted into the Pro Football Hall of Fame—just four years after he was inducted into the College Football Hall of Fame.

Floridians Love the Rodeo

When you think of the rodeo, the Sunshine State might not be the first that comes to mind. But Floridians love the rodeo!

There are a number of popular rodeos held throughout the state. These include:

Ram National Circuit Finals Rodeo

This rodeo, which consists of seven major rodeo events, has been going on for 31 years, as of 2018! Though the rodeo's location has changed states over the years, it's currently located at the Silver Spurs Arena in Kissimmee, Florida, the top two contestants from the other 12 rodeo circuits will compete. Meaning, only winners from the other 12 circuits get to compete in the rodeo. For most of the competitors, this is the largest rodeo they will ever get the chance to compete in throughout the course of their careers.

The winner earns $1 million in cash and other prizes. This is the highest-paid rodeo in the state of Florida.

The livestock at Ram National Circuit Finals Rodeo is considered the "top stock" in the country. It's brought to the rodeo each year from up to 18 different stock contractors. The RNCFR is one of only two radios in the entire country to feature as much livestock.

Silver Spurs Rodeo

The Silver Spurs Rodeo, which is hosted by the Silver Spurs Riding club, takes place two times a year. Like Ram National Circuit Finals Rodeo, the event is held in Kissimmee at the Silver Spurs Arena.

The rodeo has been called "the largest rodeo East of the Mississippi." Not only does it feature all seven major rodeo events, but it also hosts a specialty act and a kids' calf scramble. Most of the best contestants are local, but the event does draw in people throughout the United States because of the high purse amount.

The livestock featured at this rodeo is primarily produced by the Silver Spurs Club, though some livestock may be brought in.

Rodeo competitors only compete once during the event. Winners are announced at the end of the day of each competition.

Arcadia All-Florida Championship Rodeo

The Arcadia rodeo is the oldest in the Sunshine State. The event has been taking place every year since 1952, though its origins date back to 1929 when American Legion members held their first rodeo. Over the years, the rodeo has gone from cowboys and ranchers showing off their skills to provide entertainment to local competitors to a championship rodeo.

The rodeo committee contracts the best livestock from three contractors.

Rodeo contestants compete each year for about $100,000.

The Arcadia All-Florida Championship Rodeo is one of the largest rodeos to be held in Florida, as it draws in about 17,000 spectators every year.

Lakeland Pro Rodeo Classic

Located at the Lakeland Center every year, the Lakeland Pro Rodeo Classic is hosted by Mason Pro Rodeo Productions.

The rodeo consists of the seven major rodeo events, as well as specialty acts. Gator Boys perform at the event, which has been a huge draw.

Livestock for the event comes from 4L and Diamond S Rodeo.

While the event does sell out, it's one of the smaller rodeos in the state. You can generally expect to find 7,000 rodeo fans in the indoor arena's audience for every performance.

Okeechobee Cattleman's Spring Rodeo

This rodeo has been around since 1983. The Okeechobee Cattleman's Spring Rodeo is hosted by the local Cattleman's Association.

The event is held in an outdoor arena each year. Similar to the Silver Spurs Rodeo, competitors only get one go-round, meaning you'll only see each contestant once. Most of the contestants are usually local and they compete in all seven events, competing for a purse amount of about $40,000.

There's plenty for rodeo fans to do at this event. They can watch specialty acts, including Wild Child, do the calf scramble, and also check out the local fair that happens at the same time as the rodeo.

Livestock for the event is generally provided by 5 Star Rodeo and Silver Spurs Club. The cattle typically come from 5 Star.

If you have an interest in the rodeo, there are plenty of great options in the Sunshine State!

Hall of Famers Have Played for the Miami Heat

Did you know that a few Miami Heat players have gone on to be inducted into the Naismith Memorial Basketball Hall of Fame?

Those players were:

- **Shaquille O'Neal** – Nicknamed "Shaq," Shaquille O'Neal is regarded as one of the best basketball players in the history of the NBA. Shaq was one of the heaviest players to ever play for the NBA at 325 pounds and 7'1". O'Neal set a number of records throughout the course of his basketball career, including being one of only three players in the NBA to win the league's MVP. In 2016, Shaq was inducted into the Naismith Memorial Basketball Hall of Fame. The following year, he was inducted into the FIBA Hall of Fame.

- **Alonzo Mourning** – Former NBA player Mourning played the majority of his basketball career for the Miami Heat. Not only did the Heat set a record of 61 wins in one season while Mourning was on the team, but when Mourning returned from retirement after his kidney transplant, he helped the team set the 2nd best record in the NBA Eastern conference in 2004-2005. In 2009, Mourning was the first player in Miami Heat history to ever have his jersey number retired and, in 2014, was inducted into the Basketball Hall of Fame.

- **Gary Payton** – Payton, who was known as "The Glove" due to his defensive skills, ended his professional basketball career with the Miami Heat. Payton won an NBA championship while he was a part of the Heat. He is viewed as one of the best point guards of all time. He also holds the record as the only point guard who has won the award for NBA Defensive Player of the Year. Payton became a Hall of Famer in 2013.

Florida is Where MLB Teams Do Their Spring Training

You've probably heard that you have a good chance of running into athletes while you're in Florida. This is because many sports teams, including the MLB, do their spring training in the Sunshine State.

Here's a list of MLB teams and the stadiums where they do their spring training:

- The New York Yankees train at George M. Steinbrenner Field in Tampa
- The Boston Red Sox train at JetBlue Park at Fenway South in Fort Myers
- The New York Mets train at First Data Field in Port St. Lucie
- The Philadelphia Phillies train at Spectrum Field in Clearwater

- The Atlanta Braves train at Champion Stadium in Lake Buena Vista
- The Tampa Bay Rays train at Charlotte Sports Park in Port Charlotte
- The Baltimore Orioles train at Ed Smith Stadium in Sarasota
- The Minnesota Twins train at Hammond Stadium in Fort Myers
- The Detroit Tigers train at Joker Marchant Stadium in Lakeland
- The Toronto Blue Jays train at Dunedin Stadium in Dunedin
- The Pittsburgh Pirates train at LECOM Park in Bradenton
- The Houston Astros train at the Fitteam Ballpark of the Palm Beaches in West Palm Beach
- The Miami Marlins train at Roger Dean Stadium in Jupiter

The Super Bowl Was Hosted in Florida 10 Times

The Super Bowl has been played in Florida a total of 10 times over the years! Here's a list of the Super Bowls that have been held in the Sunshine State:

1. Super Bowl II in 1968 – Packers, Raiders: 33-14
2. Super Bowl III in 1969 – Jets, Colts: 16-7
3. Super Bowl V in 1971 – Colts, Cowboys – 16, 13
4. Super Bowl X in 1976 – Steelers, Cowboys: 21-17
5. Super Bowl XIII in 1979 – Steelers, Cowboys: 35-31

6. Super Bowl XXIII in 1989 – 49ers, Bengals: 20-16
7. Super Bowl XXIX in 1995 – 49ers, Chargers: 49, 26
8. Super Bowl XXXIII in 1999 – Broncos, Falcons: 34-19
9. Super Bowl XLI in 2007 – Colts, Bears: 29-17
10. Super Bowl XLIV in 2010 – Saints, Colts: 31-17

The Super Bowl is also set to be played in South Florida in 2020!

Florida Hosts an Annual World-Famous Surfing Competition

With its beautiful beaches and nice weather, it's not surprising that Florida hosts an annual surfing competition.

The O'Neill Sebastian Inlet Pro, known as the SI Pro, is recognized globally. It has been the jumpstart for the international professional surfing season for half a decade.

The competition is held by Ron Jon Surf Shop at the Space Coast in Florida. It's the largest sporting event in East Central Florida. In fact, 24,000 people attended the 2008 competition.

The event is a 4-star WQS event. Each year, around 200 surfers compete for both WQS points and money in the amount of more than $80,000.

The Red Bull Tow-At is also held during the

competition. During this event, 10 people are invited to be pulled by a Sea-Doo watercraft into the surf at high speeds. Competitors, who attempt to make miraculous moves during the event, will have a chance at winning a watercraft of their own.

Mitch Varnes of Board Sports Management, Inc. founded and currently owns both the SI Pro competition and the Red Bull Tow-At.

In 2005, Kelly Slate, who earned the seventh World Tour title, won 2nd place in the O'Neill Sebastian Inlet Pro. Some other notable winners of the competition include Damien Hobgood, C.J. Hobgood, and Patrick Gudauskas.

Florida is Home to the World Golf Hall of Fame

When you think about golf and Florida, there's a chance that President Donald Trump might come to mind. However, there may be a good reason the president loves to go golfing in the Sunshine State. There are more than 1,300 golf courses in all of Florida, which is more than any other state in the entire country. In addition to being a hotspot among golf players, Florida is also home to the World Golf Hall of Fame.

Located in St. Augustine, the World Golf Hall of Fames honors legendary golfers and preserves the history of the sport. Some of its exhibits include "Nancy Lopez:

Pride, Passion & Personality," "Bob Hope: Shanks for the Memory," "Honoring the Legacy: A Tribute to African-Americans in Golf," "Major Moments: Celebrating Golf's Greatest Championships," "Road to Rio: Golf's Return to the Olympics," and "Arnold Palmer: A Life Well Played." There's also the World Golf Hall of Fame IMAX Theater, which airs both educational programs and Hollywood movies in a 3D theater.

RANDOM FACTS

1. The Daytona 500 attracts a *huge* audience. The number of NASCAR fans in attendance varies, but the speedway holds more than 101,000 people and the event generally sells out or gets extremely close to selling out.

2. NASCAR doesn't release how much the winners take home from the Daytona 500. The prize money allegedly varies. That being said, whoever hits the top spot at the Daytona 500 is said to net the winning team a million dollars. In 2015, $18 million was awarded to *all* of the teams.

3. Babe Ruth's longest home run, which is often referred to as "Babe's Longest Homer," took place in Florida! It took place in 1919 at Plant Field stadium in Tampa, which was where spring training was held. Babe Ruth, who then played for the Boston Red Sox, hit a ball that sailed 587 feet.

4. The Miami Dolphins were founded in 1966. The co-founders of the team were Joe Robbie, an attorney/politician, and actor Danny Thomas.

5. The Miami Dolphins got their name as the result of a contest, which almost 20,000 people entered. According to the team's website, when the winner

was announced in October of 1965, Joe Robbie said, "The dolphin is one of the fastest and smartest creatures of the sea. Dolphins can attack and kill a shark or a whale. Sailors say bad luck will come to anyone who harms one of them."

6. As of 2013, the Miami Dolphins are owned by real estate developer Stephen M. Ross. Since he became the owner of the team, Ross has added several minority team owners, which include Serena and Venus Williams, Marc Anthony, and Gloria Estefan.

7. Don Shula was the Miami Dolphins' coach in 1972 and 1973. Those years, the Miami Dolphins played—and won—in the Super Bowl.

8. Miami Dolphins defensive tackle Ndamukong Suh broke a record in 2015 when he became the highest paid defensive player in the history of the NFL. Suh signed a contract for $114 million.

9. Deion Sanders, who grew up in Fort Myers, is considered one of the best U.S. athletes in history. Sanders attended Fort Myers high school where he was an All-State honoree in football. While Sanders played both professional football and baseball, his career could have gone in a different direction. The Kansas City Royals selected him for the MLB draft, but Sanders didn't sign with them. Instead, Deion Sanders attended Florida State

University where he played football, baseball, and track for the Florida State Seminoles. In 1988, he signed with the New York Yankees. By 1989, however, he signed with the NFL's Atlanta Falcons, who he played with until 1993.

10. Known as the best switch hitter of all times, Chipper Jones was born in DeLand, Florida. He attended Taylor High School and later Bolles School in Jacksonville. He was the primary third baseman for the Atlanta Braves from 1995 to 2012. In 2018, Chipper Jones was inducted into the National Baseball Hall of Fame.

11. A lot of Florida Gators get drafted by the NFL. In 1978, the highest number of Gators were drafted during one season. Ten Gators were drafted by the NFL that season. There were three other seasons where nine players were also drafted.

12. The Florida Gators has appeared in 10 SEC Championship Games. This is more than any other team in college football. The team played in the first five SEC Championship Games. Four of those games were against Alabama, while one was against Arkansas. The Florida Gators have won eight out of the 10 SEC Championship Games they've played in. The team won its first official SEC Championship in 1991 when they were led by Steve Spurrier.

13. The NHL team the Tampa Bay Lightning got their name due to Tampa being the "Lightning Capital of North America." This wasn't the only team name that was suggested. Team founder Phil Esposito said the Tampa Bay Pelicans was mentioned (but he felt it was too "girly") and the Tampa Bay Gators was also suggested, but they couldn't use it because of the Florida Gators.

14. Considered the all-time greatest defensive tackle, Warren Sapp came from Florida. He was born in Orlando and raised in Plymouth. Sapp attended Apopka High School where he played multiple football positions. While he was in high school, he tackled future MLB player Johnny Damon and gave him a concussion. After high school, Sapp played football for the University of Miami before going on to be drafted by the Tampa Bay Buccaneers.

15. Former NFL player Ray Lewis, who's considered one of the greatest defensive players of all time, was born in Bartow, Florida. He attended the University of Miami, where he played football for the Hurricanes. He was later drafted by the Baltimore Ravens. Throughout his 17-year career, he was one of the most feared defensive players. Not only did Lewis play in the Pro Bowl 13 times, but he's one of the only NFL players to have played in the bowl during three different decades (the 1990s, 2000s, and 2010s).

16. Former NFL player Michael Irvin attended St. Thomas Aquinas High School, where he was a star football player. He was recruited by the Miami Hurricanes. While he was playing for the Miami Hurricanes, they had one of the most dominant college teams of all time. Irvin was known to be one of the best wide receivers in the NFL during the course of his career, which led him to be inducted into the Pro Football Hall of Fame in 2007.

17. Legendary golf player Tiger Woods currently resides in Jupiter Island, Florida. After his divorced, he moved into the $39 million property he had purchased with his wife when they were still together.

18. The Miami Hurricanes' official sports mascot was a 65-pound brown and white boxer dog. Not entirely sure what the team mascot has to do with the team name, but alrighty then!

19. The Florida Gators and the Miami Hurricanes have a longstanding football rivalry that dates back to 1944 when the two teams started playing one another annually. During those times, the winning team would take home the Seminole War Canoe Trophy. Since 1987, the game is no longer played each year—though there's still a rivalry between Gators and Hurricanes fans. Today, the winner of Florida's three big college football teams (the

Florida Gators, the Miami Hurricanes, and the Florida State Seminoles) is awarded with the Florida Cup. The Miami Hurricanes have won the most times.

20. Florida is Home to the World's Longest River Sailboat Race. The Annual Mug Race of Florida, which was established in 1954, encompasses 35 miles. Racers will sail down the St. Johns River, with the course beginning in Palatka and ending in Jacksonville. Thousands of sailors have competed in the race, even during less than ideal weather conditions. Contestants compete for the Mug or to win one of the 50 class trophies.

Test Yourself – Questions and Answers

1. Which former Miami Dolphins player is regarded as one of the best quarterbacks of all time is?

    a. Dan Marino
    b. Tim Tebow
    c. Emmett Smith

2. The world's longest ___ race takes place in Florida.

    a. Kayak
    b. Airboat
    c. River sailboat

3. Which legendary NASCAR star died at the Daytona 500?

    a. Jeff Gordon
    b. Dale Earnhardt
    c. Jimmie Johnson

4. Florida is home to which of the following?

    a. The Pro Football Hall of Fame
    b. The National Baseball Hall of Fame
    c. The World Golf Hall of Fame

5. Which sports foundation was founded in Florida?

    a. NASCAR
    b. NFL
    c. NBA

Answers

1. a.
2. c.
3. b.
4. c.
5. a.

DON'T FORGET YOUR
FREE BOOKS

OTHER BOOKS IN THIS SERIES

Are you looking to learn more about Texas? Sure, you've heard about the Alamo and JFK's assassination in history class, but there's so much about the Lone Star State that even natives don't know about. In this trivia book, you'll journey through Texas's history, pop culture, sports, folklore, and so much more!

In The Great Book of Texas, some of the things you will learn include:

Which Texas hero isn't even from Texas?

Why is Texas called the Lone Star State?

Which hotel in Austin is one of the most haunted hotels in the United States?

Where was Bonnie and Clyde's hideout located?

Which Tejano musician is buried in Corpus Christi?

What unsolved mysteries happened in the state?

Which Texas-born celebrity was voted "Most Handsome" in high school?

Which popular TV show star just opened a brewery in Austin?

You'll find out the answers to these questions and many other facts. Some of them will be fun, some of them will creepy, and some of them will be sad, but all of them will be fascinating! This book is jampacked with everything you could have ever wondered about Texas.

Whether you consider yourself a Texas pro or you know absolutely nothing about the state, you'll learn something new as you discover more about the state's past, present, and future. Find out about things that weren't mentioned in your history book. In fact, you might even be able to impress your history teacher with your newfound knowledge once you've finished reading! So, what are you waiting for? Dive in now to learn all there is to know about the Lone Star State!

Want to learn more about New York? Sure, you've heard about the Statue of Liberty, but how much do you really know about the Empire State? Do you know why it's even called the Empire State? There's so much about New York that even state natives don't know. In this trivia book, you'll learn more about New York's history, pop culture, folklore, sports, and so much more!

In The Great Book of New York, you'll learn the answers to the following questions:

- Why is New York City called the Big Apple?
- What genre of music started out in New York City?
- Which late actress's life is celebrated at a festival held in her hometown every year?
- Which monster might be living in a lake in New York?

- Was there really a Staten Island bogeyman?
- Which movie is loosely based on New York in the 1800s?
- Which cult favorite cake recipe got its start in New York?
- Why do the New York Yankees have pinstripe uniforms?

These are just a few of the many facts you'll find in this book. Some of them will be fun, some of them will be sad, and some of them will be so chilling they'll give you goosebumps, but all of them will be fascinating! This book is full of everything you've ever wondered about New York.

It doesn't matter if you consider yourself a New York state expert or if you know nothing about the Empire State. You're bound to learn something new as you journey through each chapter. You'll be able to impress your friends on your next trivia night!

So, what are you waiting for? Dive in now so you can learn all there is to know about New York!

Are you interested in learning more about California? Sure, you've heard of Hollywood, but how much do you really know about the Golden State? Do you know how it got its nickname or what it was nicknamed first? There's so much to know about California that even people born in the state don't know it all. In this trivia book, you'll learn more about California's history, pop culture, folklore, sports, and so much more!

In The Great Book of California, you'll discover the answers to the following questions

- Why is California called the Golden State?
- What music genres started out in California?
- Which celebrity sex icon's death remains a mystery?
- Which serial killer once murdered in the state?
- Which childhood toy started out in California?

- Which famous fast-food chain opened its first location in the Golden State?
- Which famous athletes are from California?

These are just a few of the many facts you'll find in this book. Some of them will be entertaining, some of them will be tragic, and some of them may haunt you, but all of them will be interesting! This book is full of everything you've ever wondered about California and then some!

Whether you consider yourself a California state expert or you know nothing about the Golden State, you're bound to learn something new in each chapter. You'll be able to impress your college history professor or your friends during your next trivia night!

What are you waiting for? Get started to learn all there is to know about California!

MORE BOOKS BY BILL O'NEILL

I hope you enjoyed this book and learned something new. Please feel free to check out some of my previous books on <u>Amazon.</u>

Made in the USA
Middletown, DE
01 February 2020

84024647R00106